Play Matters

Playful Thinking

Jesper Juul, Geoffrey Long, and William Uricchio, editors

The Art of Failure: An Essay on the Pain of Playing Video Games, Jesper Juul, 2013

Uncertainty in Games, Greg Costikyan, 2013

Play Matters, Miguel Sicart, 2014

Play Matters

Miguel Sicart

The MIT Press
Cambridge, Massachusetts
London, England

MIT Press books may be purchased at special quantity discounts for business or sales promotional use. For information, please email special_sales@mitpress.mit.edu.

This book was set in Stone by the MIT Press. Printed and bound in the United States of America.

Library of Congress Cataloging-in-Publication Data

Sicart, Miguel, 1978–
Play matters / Miguel Sicart.
    p.   cm. — (Playful thinking)
Includes bibliographical references and index.
ISBN 978-0-262-02792-2 (hardcover : alk. paper)
1. Play—Psychological aspects. I. Title.
BF717.S49   2014
155—dc23
2014003660

10   9   8   7   6   5   4   3   2   1

Contents

On Thinking Playfully

Many people (we series editors included) find video games exhilarating, but it can be just as interesting to ponder why that is so. What do video games do? What can they be used for? How do they work? How do they relate to the rest of the world? Why is play both so important and so powerful?

Playful Thinking is a series of short, readable, and argumentative books that share some playfulness and excitement with the games that they are about. Each book in the series is small enough to fit in a backpack or coat pocket, and combines depth with readability for any reader interested in playing more thoughtfully or thinking more playfully. This includes, but is by no means limited to, academics, game makers, and curious players.

So, we are casting our net wide. Each book in our series provides a blend of new insights and interesting arguments with overviews of knowledge from game studies and other areas. You will see this reflected not just in the range of titles in our series, but in the range of authors creating them. Our basic assumption is simple: video games are such a flourishing medium that any new perspective on them is likely to show us something unseen or forgotten, including those from such unconventional voices as artists, philosophers, or specialists in other industries or fields of study. These books are bridge builders, cross-pollinating both areas with new knowledge and new ways of thinking.

At its heart, this is what Playful Thinking is all about: new ways of thinking about games and new ways of using games to think about the rest of the world.

Jesper Juul
Geoffrey Long
William Uricchio

Acknowledgments

This book has given me the excuse to meet, work with, learn from, and teach many great people. First of all, it has given me the opportunity to work again with Doug Sery and the MIT Press crew, always a pleasure. The editors of the Playful Thinking series, Jesper Juul, Geoffrey Long, and especially William Uricchio, were of invaluable help in shaping this book. I am also indebted to the anonymous reviewers who helped me improve the book in critical ways.

This book was inspired by and owes much to TL Taylor and Doug Wilson. Gonzalo Frasca, Bart Simon, Jaako Stenros, and Olli Leino have been sources of inspiration—and of challenges too.

The structure of the book crystallized when I was teaching a design course in playful interaction at the IT University of Copenhagen in 2011. I am thankful for my students' patience.

I thank as well the organizers of the Copenhagen Play Festival (w00t.dk), especially Thomas Vigild and the Copenhagen Game Collective, who gave me the opportunity to present a short version of this book during the 2013 festival.

Play Matters benefited from a number of readers who helped with the early drafts of this text: you know who you are and how much I appreciate your help. Sebastian Deterding and Sebastian Möring especially contributed with productive criticism and insights.

Finally, Ane provides help, support, and a smile when I most need it.

This book is for Carlos and Silas, makers of chaos and order in play.

Instructions for Reading This Book

Look at the number of notes in this book.

There are *hundreds* of them. (Yes, you read right.) But don't despair. You can read *Play Matters* without reading any of the notes. They will be there, waiting for you—perhaps even haunting you. But you do not need to read them.

If you want to know more about play and why it matters, go ahead and read the text. Ignore the notes until you find an idea that provokes you or puzzles you or is a concept you want to know more about. The notes are there to expand the book and give you other ideas, other perspectives, other challenges.

The notes are an extension of the book, and so is the book's website, playmatters.cc. Use them to explore beyond the bounds of this book why play matters.

1 Play Is

Think about play, and what it means to you.

What comes to mind? A pastime? Games? Childhood activities? The opposite of work? A source for learning? What you'd rather be doing now?

Think again: How much do you know about play?

Let's start with a simple exercise. List your daily activities, the tasks that structure your day, from work to leisure to those things you have to do that are neither, yet you *have to* do them.

How do you do these tasks? If you are happy and well rested, you may approach your day in a playful way, enjoying what you do. Happiness may give you time to play, to live in a different way. The temptation of enjoying and living life through play, of having fun, is always present.

To play is to be in the world. Playing is a form of understanding what surrounds us and who we are, and a way of engaging with others. Play is a mode of being human.

We live in exciting times. You might have encountered the argument that games are now everywhere[1]; that intellectuals, artists, policymakers, and institutions are games for serious and trivial purposes. You might have also read that games will be "the dominant cultural form of the XXI Century."[2] There is even talk among game developers of the twenty-first century being "the ludic [as in, play-centric] century."[3]

I disagree, to a certain extent. Games don't matter. Like in the old fable, we are the fools looking at the finger when someone points at the moon. Games are the finger; play is the moon.

What is true is that play is a dominant way of expression in our First World societies. We play games, but also *with* toys, *on* playgrounds, *with* technologies and design. And play is not just the ludic, harmless, encapsulated, and positive activity that philosophers have described.[4] Like any other form of being, play can be dangerous; it can be hurting, damaging, antisocial, corrupting. Play is a manifestation of humanity, used for expressing and being in the world.

To understand what play is, I propose here a portable theory, or rhetoric, of play. Instead of deriving an understanding of play from a particular object or activity, like war, ritual, or games, I see play as a portable tool for being. It is not tied to objects but brought by people to the complex interrelations with and between things that form daily life.

Why propose a theory of play now? In our culture, *playful* has become a positive word. The author of the 2011 biography of Steve Jobs uses *playful* as a word of praise for the design of Apple computers, originally conceived to contrast with dull corporate machines.[5] Apple's "playful" design appropriated cues from an understanding of play as a personal expression: beauty, countercultural politics, and moral values. That is the value and place of play in our culture.

Despite its importance, we are still trying to understand play with models inherited from the past. Our theories are mostly derived from the work of Dutch cultural historian Johan Huizinga, who famously coined the concept of Homo Ludens.[6] This book is not written in the tradition of Huizingan play, understood as a fair contest that creates a separate world with rules that are never questioned. The nature of play I am advocating for here is different from that of Huizinga.

I am not going to oppose play to reality, to work, to ritual or sports because it exists in all of them. It is a way of being in the world, like languages, thought, faith, reason, and myth.[7]

And play is not necessarily fun. It is pleasurable, but the pleasures it creates are not always submissive to enjoyment, happiness, or positive traits. Play can be pleasurable when it hurts, offends, challenges us and teases us, and even when we are not playing. Let's not talk about play as fun but as pleasurable, opening us to the immense variations of pleasure in this world.

Play can be dangerous too:[8] it can be addicting and destructive and may lead to different types of harm—physical injuries, lost friendships, emotional breakdowns. Play is a dance between creation and destruction, between creativity and nihilism. Playing is a fragile, tense activity, prone to breakdowns. Individual play is a challenge to oneself, to keep on playing. Collective play is a balancing act of egos and interests, of purposes and intentions. Play is always on the verge of destruction, of itself and of its players, and that is precisely why it matters. Play is a movement between order and chaos.[9] Like tragedy, it fulfills its expressive purpose when it manages a fragile, oscillating balance between both. This echoes the concept of dark play,[10] exploring the boundaries between play and not play, between performance and secrecy.[11] Dark play, with its potential dangers and exhilarating results, is another example of the nature of play as a way of being in the world—a dangerous one.

Play is carnivalesque too.[12] Play appropriates events, structures, and institutions to mock them and trivialize them, or make them deadly serious. The carnival of the Middle Ages, with its capacity to subvert conventions and institutions in a suspension of time and power,[13] was a symptom of freedom.[14] Carnivalesque play takes control of the world and gives it to the players for them to explore, challenge, or subvert. It exists; it is part of the world it turns upside down. Through carnivalesque play, we express ourselves, taking over the world to laugh at it and make sense of it too.

Think about the famous Twitter bot-not-bot *horse_ebooks*.[15] Initially a spam bot, then a piece of automatic found art, and finally a piece of performance art, *Horse_ebooks* is the perfect example of carnivalesque—dangerous play and playfulness in this age of computing machinery. By taking over a social situation and technology, this (not)-bot-come-art piece played with our expectations, broke our hearts, and showed us a new way of seeing the world and understanding ourselves. *Horse_ebooks* was appropriated by a performance artist to explore new horizons by impersonating a twitter bot in Marina Abramovic-inspired durational arts. By faking being a bot, the artist Jacob Bakkila teased our perception of Twitter and the technologies to which we relinquish our entertainment. The sense of betrayal that some felt when *Horse_ebooks* was revealed to be human can be understood only as an example of carnivalesque dark play and the ways in which it can painfully enrich our lives.

This is also not a theory of play *through* games. Games don't matter that much. They are a manifestation, a form of and for play, just not the only one. They are the strongest form, culturally and economically dominant. But they are part of an ecology of playthings and play contexts, from toys to playgrounds, from political action to aesthetic performance, through which play is used for expression. This book explores this ecology, from conventional computer and board games to sports, activism, critical engineering, interaction design, toys, and playgrounds. Play is the force that ties these cultural expressions together and makes them matter.

I am aware of both my ambition and the obvious limitations of what I can do. Mine is a romantic theory (or rhetoric) of play, based on an idea of creativity and expression that has been developed in the highly postromantic cultural environment of the early twenty-first century[16]. I write this theory of play as a reaction to the instrumentalized, mechanistic thinking on play championed by postmodern culture industries. This is a theory that acts as a call to playful arms, an invocation of play as a struggle against efficiency, seriousness, and technical determinism.[17]

If and when this era passes, my theory will be rendered obsolete. But right now, we need to think about play matters and reclaim play as a way of expression, a way of engaging with the world—not as an activity of consumption but as an activity of production. Like literature, art, song, and dance; like politics and love and math, play is a way of engaging and expressing our being in the world.

In fact, play is a fundamental part of our moral well-being, of the healthy and mature and complete human life. Through play we experience the world, we construct it and we destroy it, and we explore who we are and what we can say. Play frees us from moral conventions but makes them still present, so we are aware of their weight, presence, and importance.

We need play precisely because we need occasional freedom and distance from our conventional understanding of the moral fabric of society. Play is important because we need to see values and practice them and challenge them so they become more than mindless habits.

We play because we are human, and we need to understand what makes us human,[18] not in an evolutionary or cognitive way but in a humanistic way. Play is the force that pulls us together. It is a way of explaining the world, others, and ourselves. Play is expressing ourselves—who we want to be, or who we don't want to be. Play is what we do when we are human.

....

So what *is* play?

For a long time, my day has been structured around play. Lego bricks and toy cars precede my breakfast, as *Drop7* and *SpellTower* lull me to sleep; *Noby Noby Boy* helps me wait by the printer, and *Desert Bus* accompanies me in academic meetings. My life takes place in the time between play. This is perhaps the reason I believe that play articulates time—that a day, a week, a month, and a year are just arbitrary segments that we use to keep track of the times we play.

Let me foolishly try to define what play is.[19] Play, like any other human activity, is highly resistant to formalized understanding. Since I will fail too in trying to define it, I want to do so with a minimal definition of play, aware of its own fragile connection with a present time.[20] Let's start, then, by understanding what play is.

Play is contextual.[21] In a colloquial understanding of play, that context of play is the formally bound space determined by the rules and the community of play. But context is more complicated; it's a messier network of people, rules, negotiations, locations, and objects. Play happens in a tangled world of people, things, spaces, and cultures.

An obvious example is provided by sports. The laws of soccer determine the space in which the game should be officially played: a "natural or artificial" surface, "according to the rules of the competition" (law 1). But if we are to understand semiprofessional soccer, the context should also include the stadium or training grounds open to spectators, as well as the location of the grounds in the larger urban space. It is not the same to play pickup games of soccer in poor neighborhoods as it is in more affluent ones: the materiality of the game changes, and so do the interpretations of the rules and even the play styles.[22]

Context comprises the environment in which we play, the technologies with which we play, and the potential companions of play.[23] Context is the network of things, people, and places needed for play to take place. A playground is a pure play context: a separated space devoid of any other functionality than being a context for playing. But it's also true that almost any space can become a playground.

How do we know that a particular context is a context for play? Often there are cues embedded in objects that signal that a space, thing, or collective are there to play. Masks and disguises, merry-go-rounds, and computer controllers all point to the idea that play is possible in that context. Players interpret spaces and situations as potentially open to play when they perceive those cues.[24]

Artificially created objects or situations, then, can signal play. Play happens mostly in contexts designed for that activity.[25] It is important to understand that play, unlike other forms of expression, can be designed.[26] It is not designed exclusively in the Bauhaus-inspired tradition of a creator who shapes an object for a function,[27] but in a weaker sense: designed as mediated by things created to facilitate the emergence of play.

This is why play and computers get along so well. As universal machines, computers need to have instructions designed for them so they can execute an activity. Similarly, play requires a certain element of design, material or contextual or both, so we know we can play, or we can be playful. This is why play thrives in the age of computing machinery.

A way of understanding how these contexts are designed is to think about rules. From the strictly observed rules of professional sports to the fluid and unstable rules of children's games, play and rules go together.[28] Rules are the formal instruments that allow the creation and shared identification of a context of play. All contexts of play have rules of some type.

Much has been written on the nature of rules, and it is not my intention here to explain or debate what rules are. Play is derived, mediated, and situated by the use of rules. A rule determines where we play, when we stop playing, and when we can reenter the play context. A rule is written on a piece of paper or in several lines of code, upheld by a referee or a piece of circuitry or a group of friends, or even history and spaces, like house rules.

Rules are facilitators that create a context of play, frames within which play takes place.[29] However, rules are only one element of the context of play, and not the most important. They are necessary but not sufficient for play to exist: players and a certain will to play are needed to engage in play.[30] More important, rules are not sacred.[31] They are nodes in the complex network of the context of play, servants to the action of playing. Rules are another prop that can be targeted by the transformative capacities of play.[32]

Traditionally rules have been seen as the only immutable element of play. If rules were broken, play would finish and whoever broke the rules would be morally guilty.[33] More modern takes on play see the rules as more flexible and interpretive.[34] Discussing and interpreting rules is a crucial part of the play activity. This negotiation consolidates the context of play. A key ingredient of playing is thinking, manipulating, changing, and adapting rules. Rules, servant to the context, evolve while we play to address the necessities of particular play situations.

Play is also an activity in tension between creation and destruction.[35] Play is always dangerous, dabbling with risks, creating and destroying, and keeping a careful balance between both. Play is between the rational pleasures of order and creation and the sweeping euphoria of destruction and rebirth, between the Apollonian and the Dionysiac.[36]

For Nietzsche, tragedy summed up two colliding tensions in Greek culture: the culture of order and the culture of drunken disorder, the art of sculpture and the art of music. While artists moved between both, the genre of the Greek tragedy effectively merged both. The order and sobriety of the Apollonian was tensely opposed by the embodied, passionate, irrational, and irreverent Dionysiac art.[37]

The Apollonian and Dionysiac tendencies explain how players navigate the context of play. When playing, we struggle to make sense of the world by constructing our actions within a context. That struggle is not only with the obstacles and needs that play imposes on us, but also with the permanent temptations that happen in play: the temptation of breaking the context, breaking the rules, corrupting play, or, on the opposite side, letting go of all the elements of rationality and structure and letting ourselves loose in the intoxicating pleasures of play.

Lego provides an example of this tension. When building something without following any plans or instructions, I sometimes feel the temptation to build the tallest possible structure, just to see it fall. I pile pieces on top of pieces, in precarious balance, just to reach the highest possible point. I then look at my oeuvre and push it. The pleasure of the wasted time, of the pieces scattering as they hit the floor, is the pleasure of destructive play—the Dionysiac ending to my Apollonian world building.

Play is this struggle between order and chaos, between the will to create and the will to destroy.[38] Play as an affirmation of humanity occurs because we have to strive to balance it—to tie our demons and make them coexist with our passion for order[39] without falling in the mindless focus that lures us toward structured play.[40] We play by taking only moderately seriously the Apollonian structures of the game and not letting the intoxicating destruction deprive us of the virtues of submitting to order.

How do we keep the tension between the Apollonian and the Dionysiac in order? How does play manage to explore and express without spiraling into its own destruction? In classic theories of play, the answer would be that playing is a pretense, requiring a particular attitude decoupled from reality, so it would always be possible for participants to disengage with the activity.[41] But play is not detached from the world; it lives and thrives *in* the world. So how do we play between excessive order and compulsive destruction?

Play manages that balance because it is a carnivalesque activity.[42] The carnival, as Russian philosopher Mikhail Bakhtin described it, is an outcome of the expressive capacity of play,[43] managing the careful relations between creation and destruction.[44] Bakhtin's carnival is more than the time in which the power institutions of the Middle Ages allow the common people to express themselves through satire and humor.[45] The carnival foreshadows modernity—the rise of a critical, self-aware individual, a body with a mind not subject to institutions determined from another world, but from rationality itself.[46]

Carnival lets laughter, not fun, happen. By temporarily dismissing the oppressive forces of the establishment, laughter takes over and allows for a bodily form of knowledge that creates truth, and it's free. Laughter requires freedom, an opening from the institutional world, but it also creates freedom. Modernity could be a consequence of laughter, of the possibility of expression afforded in the carnival.[47] Laughter, critical and hurting and enjoyable and deeply embodied, makes carnivals matter.

Laughter and the carnival give us an instrument against seriousness, restoring the "ambivalent wholeness" that is opposite the institutions we live in.[48] Games are an example of carnivalesque behavior that leads to a festive liberation in search from freedom, expression, and truth.[49] Some games, like *B.U.T.T.O.N.*, with its rowdy, physical performativity, or even the early *Grand Theft Auto* titles and its fascinating renderings of possible worlds, point to the importance of carnivalesque laughter in the construction and experience of play.[50] Again, the result is not fun but laughter—pleasurable but risky, and potentially harmful.

Play is carnivalesque. It finds equilibrium between creation and destruction in the embodied laughter. It also presents a number of characteristics that embody this carnivalesque tensions.

Play is appropriative, in that it takes over the context in which it exists and cannot be totally predetermined by such context.

From the context of use of a toy to a game, from a ritual to a playground, context becomes servant to the activity of playing.[51] Two physical games can serve as example: the game Ninja is often played in public spaces, from parking lots to the common areas of schools and dorms (figure 1.1).[52] The rules of Ninja are simple: players make a circle, staying at arm's length from each other. At the count of three, players make a ninja pose, palms extended. The goal of the game is to hit any other players' open palms, and only the palms. If you're hit, you have to leave the game. The game continues until only one player is left. The catch? It's a turn-based game, and only one swift move of attack and defense is allowed—no stopping, no flurry of gestures, just one move to attack or to defend in each turn. Ninja makes players take over a location, forming a circle that soon loses its form and spreads around the space, effectively conquering it. But Ninja also appropriates the space in a sociocultural way: what used to be a parking lot becomes a battlefield, reclaiming the ground for pleasure. And in the public space of a school or a workplace, Ninja can reclaim the importance of laughter to survive the long days of work and obligations. Ninja appropriates the spaces it takes place by means of its sprawling nature.

A more aesthetically oriented approach is provided by *Johan Sebastian Joust*,[53] also a physical game, in this case augmented through the use of technology: *Joust* is a nongraphics video game in which players hold a Playstation Move controller in their hands. The players' movements are determined by the tempo of music: if it is played at a high tempo, players can move quickly, and if it is played at a slow tempo, only careful movement is allowed. To win *Joust*, players need to shake any other players' controllers so much that they are eliminated. The intensity of the shaking is measured by the controllers' accelerometers and related to the tempo of the music, with the results calculated by the computer.

Joust does not appropriate the context by the sheer number of players but by a careful weaving of different aesthetic cues. The PlayStation Move controller that players wield has a glowing LED that gives players information about the state of the game.

Figure 1.1
Ninja takes over IT University. (Photo by Flickr user Joao Ramos. CC-By-NC 2.0. http://www.flickr.com/photos/joaoramos/5621465814/sizes/o/.)

Joust is also a music game, so it has to be heard, not just seen. And the game performs like a dance. Seeing *Joust* being played is like witnessing an impromptu dance with magical candlelight, reinterpreting mundane locations of play into performance spaces, mesmerizing players and spectators in a choreography of moving lights and playful exhilaration (figure 1.2).[54]

The play object, be it a game or a toy, is just a prop for play. Regardless of all the intentions and meanings embedded in the design of play objects, play will always force us to contextualize the meaning of the things involved in playing. Play appropriates the objects it uses to come into existence.[55]

Play is disruptive as a consequence of being appropriate. When it takes over the context in which play take place, it breaks the state of affairs. This is often done for the sake of laughter, for

Figure 1.2
JS Joust serious duelers. (Photo by Bennett Foddy. http://www.foddy .net.)

enjoyment, for passing pleasures. But like all other passing pleasures, play can also disruptively reveal our conventions, assumptions, biases, and dislikes. In disrupting the normal state of affairs by being playful, we can go beyond fun when we appropriate a context with the intention of playing with and within it. And in that move, we reveal the inner workings of the context that we inhabit.

An interesting example of the potential disruptiveness of play is the activist performance Camover.[56] In Camover, players are encouraged to destroy CCTV cameras in a specific urban environment and are awarded points for doing so—the points are made available and visible on a website. This political (and illegal) action uses gamelike elements, such as points or the creation of a shared play community that evaluates the players' performance, to communicate a political message. Camover disrupts the urban context through violent and dangerous play, engaging with the political situation in the urban space where the play is taking place. As an intervention through play, Camover uses the appropriative nature of play to make a commentary on social and political actions as they take place.

The disruptive nature of play allows us to understand the perils of play as well. By disrupting the context in which it takes place, play is a creative, expressive force. But this force has its dangers too. Dark play is an exploration of the wild side of play in which players decide to engage in an activity, like Camover, to force an emotional response in those who do not recognize they are actually playing.[57] The disruptiveness of play is used to shock, alarm, and challenge conventions.[58]

The disruptiveness of play can be extended to more dangerous realms too.[59] Play can disrupt our mental balance. It can be addictive through gambling, for example, buying lottery tickets or playing slot machines designed for tempting our base impulses with a calculated chain of wins and losses.[60] The disruptiveness of play means that sometimes it's not the world we look at through the lens of play but an abyss—the profound contradictions and risks that our fragile minds accept taking. If we are only mildly tempted, we become spoilsports, cheaters;[61] if we are deeply enthralled, we lose ourselves in play. Play is disruptive, and it can be dangerous through its disruptiveness.

Play is autotelic—an activity with its own goals and purposes, with its own marked duration and spaces and its own conditions for ending.[62] This is a common point with conventional understandings of play.[63] However, the boundaries of autotelic play are not formally rigid; there is no clear demarcation between the world of the game and the world at large.[64] Play is autotelic in its context, but it is also negotiated. Its autotelic nature is always being discussed and negotiated. We play by negotiating the purposes of play, how far we want to extend the influences of the play activity, and how much we play for the purpose of playing or for the purpose of personal expression.

Play has a purpose of its own, but the purpose is not fixed. Play activities can be described as diachronically or synchronically autotelic, focusing on how the purpose of play evolved though the play session or looking at what particular purpose a particular instance of play had in a particular session. We can start playing with a purpose and decide to change our goals midway, either alone or in negotiation with others. Play negotiates its autotelic goals and purposes as part of playing.

Let's look at an example: the purpose of playing a game like *Vesper.5* that allows players to make only one move a day.[65] We don't play it for the action or for the way it entertains us. *Vesper.5* gives us a ritual that is play too. We play it to explore, to learn about ourselves, because we find it interesting, because it has meaning for us and we let it in our lives every day: one move and then a twenty-four-hour wait. This exercise in patience—a game, yes, in which we play more than just the game—is also a companion, a timed excuse for playing every day. Its purpose is to exist, to let us play, and the purpose of playing with it is nothing else than just playing. Playing *Vesper.5* is also negotiating why and how we play this game.

Play is creative, in that it affords players different degrees of expression inherent in the play activity itself. Playing is both accepting the rules of the game and performing within them according to our needs, personality, and constitution of a playing community. Play is the act of creatively engaging with the world, with technologies, contexts, and objects, from games to toys and playgrounds, exploring them through ludic interaction.[66] Play creates its objects and communities. To play is to make a world, through objects, with others, for others, and for us. It is a creative way of expression, shared but ultimately personal. Play creates (itself) through objects, rules, players, situations, and spaces.

A good example of this type of expression is the development of tactics in games. When playing a game, players develop tactics, that is, temporally based interpretations of the context of play suited for particular modes of interaction toward particular goals; some of them may be a part of the game and some are purely personal. The tactics are the on-the-fly creative interpretation of a game through the activity of playing it.

Finally, *play is personal*. Even when we play with others, the effects of play are individual, attached to our own sentimental, moral, and political memories. Who we are is also who plays, the kind of person we let lose when we play. Our memories are composed of these instances of play, the victories and defeats, but also the shared moments.[67] Play is not isolated in our eventful lives; in fact, it is a string with which we tie our memories and our friendships together. Play is a trace of the character that defines us.

Play is finding expression; it is letting us understand the world and, through that understanding, challenging the establishment, leading for knowledge, and creating new ties or breaking old ones. But ultimately whatever we do in play stays with us. Play is a singularly individual experience—shared, yes, but meaningful only in the way it scaffolds an individual experience of the world. Through play, we are in the world.[68]

Play is like language—a way of being in the world, of making sense of it.[69] It takes place in a context as a balance between creation and destruction, between adherence to a structure and the pleasures of destruction.[70] Playing is freedom.[71]

Play is being in the world, through objects, toward others.[72] We play not to entertain ourselves or to learn or be alienated: we play to be, and play gives us, through its characteristics, the possibility of being. As Sartre put it, "The desire to play is fundamentally the desire to be."[73]

2 Playfulness

An iPhone is just a rectangular piece of metal, glass, and plastic; a machine with few moving parts, it does not hint at its potential functionality when it is turned off. But when it's turned on, when software appropriates the hardware,[1] an iPhone is a machine of almost limitless capabilities. It is a tiny computer equipped with a web browser, a music and video player, a gaming console, a lever, a calculator, a camera, and any other thing that Apple allows it to be.[2] An iPhone, or any other smart phone, is the ultimate toy: an empty shell ready to be modified by the power of software.

The case of smart phones illustrates not only the malleable nature of toys as playthings, but also the capacity for some objects to afford playful behaviors. But what do I mean by "playfulness"? The relation between play and playfulness, more than just a casual affair, is extremely important for understanding the ecology of play and playthings.

Many of the technologies that surround us today are somewhat invested in looking like something other what they are or what they can be. A phone does not want to be a phone but a multimedia emotional companion. A television wants to be more than a fireplace substitute: it aspires to become the grandmother that tells the bedside stories you want her to tell you whenever you want. A fridge will take care of your diet, and your computer is an expressive extension of yourself. Your espresso machine probably loves you.[3]

We live in an era dominated by emotional designs—by objects created with the intention of appealing to our senses and feelings.[4] A typical rhetoric of this postfunctional design makes technologies look and feel more playful. The many animations on the user interface of Apple computers, from the opening of a folder to the minimizing of an application (figure 2.1), are not purely functional design decisions. These user interface designs are driven by a desire to signal that the machine we are interacting with is not a serious computer but something else—something quirky and with personality that will not reject the form of expression through it but will actually encourage creativity.

Tapping on our emotional attachment to things through design is not exclusive of digital technologies. Workplaces and

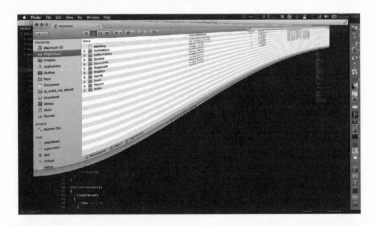

Figure 2.1
Playful user interfaces.

service providers of all kinds want to establish relations where customers or employees feel like play pals rather than mere numbers or cogs of a machine.[5] Modern corporate values are strangely resonant of ideals related to good teammates, that is, to sports and games.[6] We want our modern lives to be dynamic, engaging, and full of the expressive capacities of play.[7] But we also want them to be effective, performative, serious, and valuable.[8] We need play, but not all of it—just what attracts us, what makes us create and perform and engage, without the encapsulated singularity of play.

What we want is the attitude of play without the activity of play. We need to take the same stance toward things, the world, and others that we take during play. But we should not play; rather, we should perform as expected in that (serious) context and with that (serious) object. We want play without play. We want playfulness—the capacity to use play outside the context of play.

Playfulness is a way of engaging with particular contexts and objects that is similar to play but respects the purposes and goals of that object or context.[9] Colloquially, playfulness can be associated with flirting and seduction: we can be playful during sex, or marriage, or work, though none of those are play. We can be playful with language through satire and puns,[10] and even in the way we engage with our productive labor.[11] However, those activities are most certainly not play; they are flirting, sex, and labor, and thus they have other purposes.

There is an important distinction to be made here. Playfulness is a physical, psychological, and emotional attitude toward things, people, and situations.[12] It is a way of engaging with the world derived from our capacity to play but lacking some of the characteristics of play. Intuitively, we can feel the difference between play and playfulness. We can also have the vague idea that we can be playful even when playing. Somehow these two concepts are overlapping, but they are not referring to the same thing.

The main difference between play and playfulness is that play is an *activity*, while playfulness is an *attitude*.[13] An activity is a coherent and finite set of actions performed for certain purposes, while an attitude is a stance toward an activity—a psychological, physical, and emotional perspective we take on activities, people, and objects.

From the bully to the socially awkward, to the seducer or the curious, attitudes are somewhat similar to the frames we use to make sense of our social and cultural presence.[14] We talk about people "having an attitude," and product marketers want to change our attitudes toward forgotten brands. Attitudes are projected on the world, and the world can resist these attitudes.[15]

In this sense, playfulness is projecting some of the characteristics of play into nonplay activities. It is an attempt to engage with the world in the mode of being of play but not playing. Sometimes that means to be playful when playing. We are playful in play contexts that are very strictly typified, in which play is bound by the strong enforcement of its structures. For instance, playfulness can take place when games are played or when sports are practiced.[16] Athletes can be playful when they perform in ways that are not optimal for reaching their purpose. Many of the flourishes with which Magic Johnson adorned his basketball game were not practical and goal oriented; they were a show for the gallery, a way of enjoying the game while playing it at the highest stakes. This beautiful playfulness created a stark contrast with the serious context of professional play, making those actions more beautiful and an embodiment of the ideal of the game.

Players of a game are playful when they consciously manipulate the relative rigidity of the system. Dark play is used as a playful approach to play situations, in which the disruptive nature of play can be used to break the conventions of gentrified play contexts. An interesting example of this understanding of play comes from the story of a group of friends who have played tag for twenty-three years.[17] For a month every year, a group of old friends play a game of tag that involves, without making them players, their families, friends, and coworkers. And not only are there players who are not playing (such as wives who act as spies but cannot be It), but also players who don't know they are playing. The employers of these men did not necessarily know about the game being played and involuntarily become pawns in the game. Imagine if the people around you were in fact playing a game you were not aware of. Imagine those multiple worlds being experienced at the same time.[18]

Another case of dark playfulness could be Antonin Panenka's famous penalty shoot in the 1976 Eurocup final against West Germany. Panenka not only made a beautiful gesture when the stakes were highest, he also playfully teased the rival's goalkeeper in a stretch of what is acceptable by sportsmanship values.[19]

In our computational age, playfulness can be seen as a play-inspired revolt against the dictates of the machine. The computer, through seductive functionalities and hidden ubiquity, shapes the tasks we perform as much as we delegate to them.[20] In this context, playfulness is a carnivalesque attack on the seriousness of computers, on the system-driven thinking that gives maximum importance to the dictates and structures of a formal structure. I am not writing here about playful user experience design, but about a darker, more explorative, and expressive approach to our relations to machines. Playfulness can be a revolt, a carnivalesque exploration of the seams of the technologies that excel at performing operations but limit the expression to that which is computable.

A good example of digital playfulness is Matteo Loglio's DIY (do it yourself) project FAKE COMPUTER REAL VIOLENCE.[21] This project connects an accelerometer to a computer microcontroller in order to measure movement and respond to it, in this case by sending a command to the operative system to restart. The fun aspect is that the project should be placed in a computer case, so when the computer freezes, a physical blow to the case will take us to the restarting menu—effectively responding to our violent attack on the machine. This ironic commentary on our perception of computer failure and our common violent reactions to it playfully allows us to restart our computer by hitting a specially designed USB extension. Equipped with an accelerometer, this extension reacts to the blows of the user by restarting the computer, effectively acting on the user's violent reaction toward the machine.

Playfulness is the carnivalesque domain of the appropriation, the triumph of the subjective laughter, of the disruptive irony over rules and commands. Playfulness means taking over a world to see it through the lens of play, to make it shake and laugh and crack because we play with it. Some objects allow us to see the world through a playful lens; some contexts are more prone to playfulness than others. A classic Goffmanian example would be a Christmas dinner at a company, which is an opening for playfulness in the context of corporate life. It could be argued too that bulletin or image boards on the Internet, particularly those that have strong anonymity settings, encourage a certain playful behavior from the user—one that can range from silly YouTube videos and comments to the more interesting and complex dark play practiced on occasion in 4chan.org, an image-based bulletin board.

Playfulness glues together an ecology of playthings, situations, behaviors, and people, extending play toward an attitude for being in the world. Through playfulness, we see the world, and we also see how the world could be structured as play. Brendan Dawes's Accidental News Explorer is an app that pulls random pieces of news from different sources (figure 2.2).[22] It provides users with a single input box where they can type a keyword, and the software will find the news for them. It is hardly the most functional news reader ever developed, yet this

Figure 2.2
The Accidental News Explorer.

serendipitous approach to news forces us to look at its choices with playful astonishment: how could a machine find the news? The news can be playful too.

For the playful attitude to exist as related to the mode of being of play, it needs to share some traits with play. Since playfulness is an attitude that projects some of the characteristics of play into the world, understanding which characteristics of play constitute the playful attitude will allow us to better understand the function of playfulness in the ecology of play.

Let's start where play and playfulness diverge. Play is *auto-telic*, an activity with its own purpose. We play for the sake of playing. Since playfulness is an attitude, a projection of characteristics into an activity, it lacks the autotelic nature. Playfulness preserves the purpose of the activity it is applied to: it's a different means to the same end. If it is sex, then the pleasures of sex are the main purpose even if we are playful. If it is using a computer to write a book, the purpose is still writing regardless of how playful we are in the process. Playfulness is not autotelic because it is not an activity. Furthermore, for it to be a productive way of being in the world, it needs to respect the purpose of the activity it is applied to. Otherwise playfulness becomes a destructive force, not engaging with the activity or with the creative capacities of play.[23] Playfulness always respects the purpose of the activity for its own integrity to exist.

This does not mean that playfulness cannot be disruptive. In many cases, a playful attitude will result in a relative disruption of the state of affairs, though without destroying it. The art project My Best Day Ever, by Zach Gage, "automatically searches twitter for the phrase 'my best day ever' and then picks a tweet it likes, and re-tweeters the tweet as its own," as the author describes it.[24] My Best Day Ever is a playful commentary on Twitter, privacy, and our desire to reach out through impersonal and techno-logically mediated mechanisms. It also shows personality by selecting appropriate tweets and a certain degree of self-irony. It somehow disrupts Twitter as a medium without destroying it, revealing the self-imposed honesty of these media. The activity needs to exist, to be finished, for the playful disruptiveness to be effective. Otherwise it is just destruction, a nihilist attitude different from the creative approach that playfulness affords.

So what does playfulness bring to these other activities? Why does playfulness matter? Playfulness assumes one of the core attributes of play: appropriation. To be playful is to appropriate a context that is not created or intended for play.[25] Playfulness is the playlike appropriation of what should not be play. Brendan Dawes's DoodleBuzz is a "typographic news explorer" in which users can find news pieces by drawing doodles on the web browser canvas.[26] Again, news reading through DoodleBuzz is significantly different from reading it through a conventional news reader; however, the physicality of the interaction (drawing doodles) and the serendipity of the underlying system contribute to the playful experience. Reading news is not supposed to be physical, or drawn by chance. News reading ought to be effective, functional—unless, of course, we want our news consumption to be personal, expressive, and appropriative and to make the news ours by drawing it.

In playfulness, appropriation happens in its pure form, taking over a situation to perceive it differently, letting play be the interpretive power of that context. Appropriation implies a shift in the way a particular technology or situation is interpreted. The most usual transformation is from functional or goal oriented to pleasurable or emotionally engaging. Appropriation transforms a context by means of the attitude projected to it.

Playfulness reambiguates the world.[27] Through the characteristics of play, it makes it less formalized, less explained, open to
interpretation and wonder and manipulation. To be playful is to
add ambiguity to the world and play with that ambiguity.

In this sense, the difference between contexts needs to be
specified. Play happens in contexts created for play, in those
contexts in which the autotelic nature of play is respected.[28] Traditionally these contexts are games, but they can also be playgrounds or temporal contexts such as the lunch break: openings
in time and space where play becomes possible. The contexts in
which playfulness happens are not designed or created for play:
they are occupied by play.

We occupy contexts through playfulness to be creative or
disruptive. A PowerPoint presentation can be a dry showcase of
charts and numbers, or a dynamic visual experience of data.[29]
Similarly, data visualization has become a contemporary playground for the exploration of how data can be made significant
and more visible through playfulness. Projects like Live Plasma,[30]
a visualizing tool that helps recommend music to users, or Twitter Earth,[31] a tool that locates a tweet on a three-dimensional
representation of the globe based on the location data embedded on the tweet, are examples of playful interpretations of data.
This approach is also closely related to the aesthetics of play
and playfulness. Julian Oliver's Packet Garden visualizes network traffic by growing a world, each network package or communication activity translated into a geographical or ecological
element of that world.[32] Uploads are hills, and there are HTTP
plants and peer-to-peer plants.

These are creative appropriations of data through playfulness, revealing new knowledge through play. Playful appropriation allows for the expression of idiosyncrasies in even the most

rigid of contexts. Through playfulness, we open the possibility of expressing who we are. Even in instrumental situations, personality is tied to performance, to the fulfillment of schedules. Playfulness frees us from the dictates of purpose through the carnivalesque inheritance of play. Through playful appropriation, we bring freedom to a context.

Playfulness can be used for disruption, revealing the seams of behaviors, technologies, or situations that we take for granted. The Newstweek project literally takes over open wireless networks to playfully manipulate news consumption (by manipulating the headlines of major news providers in real time), shattering our assumptions on networks, news, and consumption of stories through online gatekeepers.[33] Similarly, Moss Graffiti can take over spaces such as parks, often carefully walled against their own users, and make them playfully public again.[34] Through playfulness, we incorporate a personal view into the situations we live in. Playfulness, like a carnival, is an opening toward critique and satire, toward freedom in the context of mundane activities.

There is one last characteristic of play that is present in the playful attitude: play is personal, and playfulness is used to imbue the functional world with personal expression. If we look at the evolution of modern personal computing, from the desktop to the mobile, we see how machines have become more flexible toward personalization. We can change screen backgrounds, or ring tones, and through them we express ourselves. The temporary popularity of using an old-fashioned ringing sound with a modern mobile phone was a way of playfully relating to the machine itself and its nature. The dissonance between technology and sound was supposed to be not only ironic but also personal.

Through playfulness we personalize the world; we make it ours while still acknowledging that it has a purpose other than playing. Through playfulness, we bring the creative and free personal expression that play affords to a world outside play, and therefore we make the world personal.

Of course, the world might resist. In fact, many situations, contexts, and objects are specifically designed to resist playfulness; the instrument panels of planes or other critical systems should not be toyed with. Regardless of the positive values we give as a society to creativity and play, there is still a tension between labor and expression, between functionality and emotions. The functional tradition in design focused on efficiency and productivity.[35] This modernist dream is Tati's nightmare in the film *Playtime*, which chronicles the slow but finally triumphant flow of play in the rationalist world of modernist France. That was a world in which technology guided people through the straps of daily production and efficiency. *Playtime* is a song of freedom, an ironic view on playfulness taking over the dullness of everyday life. That is why playfulness matters: it brings the essential qualities of freedom and personal expression to the world outside play.

The traditions in design, however, seem to focus on preventing playfulness, on resisting by design the temptation of appropriation. Even Apple computers, the most voluntarily playful of computing environments, are carefully engineered to allow only certain sanctioned types of playfulness. More than a prop for play, Apple technologies, like so many others, present themselves as a referee more than a player.

Designing playfulness is more complex than what it might seem. One of the advantages of functional design is the relative predictability of the outcome: because an object is designed with its function in mind, all of its elements are guided toward that purpose and all deviant behaviors can be minimized. Household appliances are often good examples of this, easing our daily tasks but not necessarily enhancing our experience of the mundane. When I compare my fridge or dishwasher with my computer or a car dashboard, I can see how performance is paramount to the design. I do not care about my fridge; I have no emotional feelings toward it. It is functional but not emotional.[36]

Playful designs are by definition ambiguous, self-effacing, and in need of a user who will complete them. Playful design breaks away from designer-centric thinking and puts into focus an object as a conversation among user, designer, context, and purpose. In fact, what playful design focuses on is the awareness of context as part of the design. Rather than imposing a context, playful designs open themselves to interpretation; they suggest their behaviors to their users, who are in charge of making them meaningful. Playful designs require a willing user, a comrade in play.[37]

This approach to design downplays system authority,[38] a minor but crucial revolt against the relative scientism of design, from games to word processors.[39] Playful design is personal in both the way the user appropriates it and the way the designer projects her vision into it. It's a more challenging object, a statement about rather than an acknowledgment of function. In that gap, playfulness finds its grip to appropriate the object, to make it an expression rather than a product.[40]

Playful technologies are designed for appropriation, created to encourage playfulness. These objects have a purpose, a goal, a function, but the way they reach it is through the oblique, personal, and appropriative act of playfulness. They do not become toys or pure playthings, but the behavior and attitudes toward them, the ways they redefine the contexts in which they are applied, invoke the characteristics of play.[41]

Playful technologies are mostly extreme ideas implemented in the relative safety of academic labs and blue-sky projects.[42] These are objects that work very well in controlled environments: the studio, the art gallery.[43] But playful design still has to find its place in the uncontrolled environment of everyday life. We are comfortable with functionality, with surrendering our expressive capacities to objects that seem playful but are not radically so.

One of the most interesting examples is Apple's Siri, the artificial intelligence helper. Introduced with the iPhone 4S, Siri is a voice-activated assistant that can help phone users perform mundane tasks, such as place phone calls, make appointments, or find locations. Technologically, Siri is an impressive achievement, but its playful design is even more interesting.

Siri could have been an efficient, task-driven system, a ruthless parser of voices that would neglect to recognize anything outside its instructions database. However, Siri's designers are aware of the mischievous playfulness of users, and they prepared for it. Siri has answers for marriage proposals or questions about religion and the meaning of life (figure 2.3).[44] Siri has a personality: she is quirky, ironic, even a bit dry. Siri is a playful design that breaks our expectations and gives personality to software. It is far from being an ideal playful design, because it resists extreme appropriation (users cannot program Siri, and Siri is one for all users). However, it is a successful commercial product that defies conventionalism regarding functionality and personality. By being playful, Siri becomes a companion more than a tool.[45]

Figure 2.3
Siri is a geek.

We need more objects that allow us to be playful. We need to take the capacity of appropriation and make a world that does not resist it. At stake is more than our culture of leisure or the ideal of people's empowerment; at stake is the idea that technology is not a servant or a master but a source of expression, a way of being. These designs need to exist so we can make technologies ours, and our being in the world a personal affair.

Playfulness allows us to extend the importance of play outside the boundaries of formalized, autotelic events, away from designed playthings like toys, or spaces like the playground or the stadium. It effectively allows seeing how play is a general attitude to life. Playfulness expands the ecology of play and shows its actual importance not only in the making of culture but also in the very being of human, on how being playful and playing is what defines us. We are because we play, but also because we can be playful.

3 Toys

We first get to know what toys are as children, when they are our most coveted treasures. Toys for children are hopes and refuges, aspirations and disappointments, gates and guardians. With play, we discovered toys, and in that relation we slowly became who we are. When we grow up, toys change, but we never outgrow them, because toys are the purest things for play.

Play is a constant in our lives, an activity threading our being in the world. Play should not be seen in isolation. It is not an activity that can be easily detached from its context, its consequences, or the objects and spaces created to foster and host it. That's why a study of play needs to pay attention to the objects of play, to the playthings we create. Other theories of play have focused on games as the formal manifestation of play, the privileged playthings in the ecology of play.[1] In this book, I give toys a central position in the experience of play.

To understand the ecology of play and the role of playthings in the expressive capacities of playing, we need to understand toys. Toys can help tie together play and playfulness, strengthening this ecological theory of expressive and creative play.

Much like play, any formal definition of *toy* will be incomplete.[2] I am interested in the toy as related to the type of play that matters: the expressive, creative, appropriative, and personal activity through which we make sense of the world. A toy is both a cultural object that performs a function in the ecology of play and a device created to perform that function. Toys are defined by their cultural and technical dimensions: the toy as expression and the toy as a thing.[3]

The expressive toy is an object that encourages play through appropriation of spaces, our attention, or, in the digital context, other technologies. The digital toy *Noby Noby Boy* is a humorous appropriation of smart phones (figure 3.1). *Noby Noby Boy* allows users to perform exactly the same activities as their phone affords, from e-mailing to taking pictures.[4] However, it turns these activities into toys, adding a layer of humor to playing music or chatting with friends. *Noby Noby Boy* appropriates the uses of a smart phone and turns it into a whimsical toy, a plaything that forces users to interact with a familiar device in an unaccustomed way, for example by adding a layer of silly, cute drawings to the camera visor and making the act of taking a picture both charming and much more complicated.

Play matters when it is appropriative, taking over a situation and turning it into a context of play. Toys facilitate appropriation: they create an opening in the constitution of a particular situation that justifies the activity of play. Through toys, we realize that play is possible, and we start playing. The toy is a gate to the world understood through play.

For instance, Daniel Disselkøen's Man Eater project offers a very simple toy that takes over a situation for pure fun.[5] Although Man Eater is just a simple sticker of a monster with an open mouth, attaching it to the big window of a bus or tram makes commuting a more engaging activity—the monster will eat the passers-by! They are no longer random people, but victims of the

Figure 3.1
Noby Noby Boy tells the time.

toy monster that has been unleashed! A simple sticker opens the world for play.

That opening can happen intrinsically and extrinsically. Intrinsically, the toy is cueing for an inner world of play, a parallel world that should exist only through play. Dolls, toy cars, construction sets: they foster the creation of an intrinsic, object-centric context that emanates from the toy itself. Some toys invoke play extrinsically, forcing us to take over external spaces for the purpose of play. A ball, a Frisbee, a bicycle: they modify the space in which they are used for play. Some toys open for appropriation by creating a world; others open for appropriation by occupying the world.

Noby Noby Boy can operate in both modes: when we interact with the very simple physics toy that occupies most of the screen, our attention is focused on the simple, whimsical world of *Noby Noby Boy*, full of simple shapes that bounce around at our command (figure 3.2). When we choose to take a picture through the toy or to map our travels, we are engaging with the world outside the toy *through the toy*. I might decide to bike an alternative way to work just to add more distance to the counter that comes with the toy. Or I might want to take a picture of a "serious thing," such as a fire extinguisher, just to mock it in the picture editor. By occupying our smart phone, *Noby Noby Boy* encourages play in both intrinsic and extrinsic ways.

Not all "toys" are created as toys. One of the most fascinating capacities humans have is being able to toy around with almost any object they can find. From pebbles to tree branches, to more complex technological objects, humans seem to enjoy playing with things, using them in ways other than those expected, intended, or recommended. We use our hands, our body, to appropriate an object and explore its functionalities and meaning

Figure 3.2
Noby Noby Boy and its interpretation of a clock.

in ways often unexpected. We spin the pen, make a ball of a piece of trash, and invent ways in which a phone or a computer can be entertaining. Anything can be turned into a toy.

This possibility derives from the appropriative nature of the playful attitude, allowing us to transform any object in an instrument for playful behavior. In fact, playful designs could be described as somewhat successful toy designs, that is, as objects that by design allow users to toy around with them. Remember why Apple's Siri is interesting: it invites us to ask silly questions, if only because we know that we might get some silly answers.

When we turn an object into a toy, we make it an instrument for either playing or a playful attitude. When we are playing, anything can become a toy. The object retains some of its original purpose and characteristics, but we access, interpret, and interact with them quite differently. Playfulness makes the performance of actions more ludic, and their instruments closer to toys. Playfulness makes the world a toy.

Toys are instruments for play and playfulness. They are either created to play or interpreted through the playful attitude. Toys also play a cultural role in the way we play and in how play is personal. A toy is an opening for appropriation. In childhood, the toy is an element for getting the fantasy started, a gate to the world of imagination. The toy becomes an extension of the playful mind, an exploration of both who we are, as children, and what we do. The child's toy waits for us on the shelves, static, promising play, and when we grab it, play takes over through the toy, and the life of imagination fills in the appropriated reality. Toys are excuses for playing, embodiments of play.

Mechanical toys, as well as autonomous toys, hold a different promise, a different type of fascination.[6] The mechanical toy and its close relative, the procedural toy (understood in a narrow sense as those mechanical toys implemented with computers and focused on simulating systems), are paradoxical objects that put their users in the double role of performer and voyeur.[7] Mechanical and procedural toys are fascinating because they don't require us; they seem to be playing on their own. We play with them to see how they behave, how they react. *Sim City* is a magnificent spectacle, a toy that can operate on its own while tempting us to tinker with its parameters to both see and understand what happens—and all the while, creating a feeling of otherness, a playful microcosm that we, as observers and tinkerers, want not to inhabit but to observe.

Mechanical and procedural toys are more than instruments; they are play pals, companions in the activity of play. We imagine the ways in which these toys play, the ways in which they, on their own, appropriate the world.[8] If playing is making sense of the world, to play with a procedural toy is to understand how an object makes sense of the world.[9]

For instance, Golan Levin's Yellowtail, which claims to be "an interactive software system for the gestural creation and performance of real-time abstract animation," can also be understood as a software toy that fascinates us with its own creations: we set it in motion, and whatever happens afterward is for us to wonder and enjoy.[10] With Yellowtail, any gesture on the surface of the screen is translated to a procedurally generated animation that we can observe. Yellowtail makes the screen not a canvas but a window to a type of alien existence within computerized parameters. Yellowtail is a play pal, encouraging us to play again and try different things, then rewarding us for doing so.

This idea of the toy as the object that cues appropriation is not new. In fact, it is at the core of the modern understanding of toys, a cultural history that has arguably taken us from the dependence on others to more solitary types of play.[11] Historically the toy has slowly evolved from a communal object for play to an individual source of pleasure. Of course, this is related to the toy as one of the fundamental instruments of the Enlightenment educational revolution.[12] Through toys, children learn not only to play but also to perform repetitive actions and understand how the processes of the world work.[13] A toy kitchen or a model car are visions of how mundane activities like cooking and transportation may work, including the conflictive gender stereotypes embedded in these objects. Toys often uncritically reflect and reproduce the mundane, so it can be learned and assimilated.

Toys are also the physical embodiment of play's freedoms. They might hint, suggest, or even demand particular forms of interaction, but a toy has no way of enforcing behaviors. Unlike games or rituals, which lead to more formalized play, toys are enablers, vehicles for play.[14] Much like playful designs, toys excel when they are ambiguous, open for interpretation—that is, when they are relatively empty vessels with which stories, worlds, and actions are constructed. A ball is just a sphere, but it contains infinite games; the Lego bricks, while designed to work in only a limited number of ways, still allow such a large number of combinations that it is not possible to say that they are directing play but encouraging it.

A toy is an opening for appropriation that suggests playing. It is the ultimate prop for play, a device that in its own relative emptiness allows play to take form, to be related to the imagination.[15] A toy is a tool for play, a thing at the service of playing and the playful—and so it is an instrument for self-expression, self-knowledge, and exploration.

These physical and cultural properties are a consequence of their design. A toy is a technology for play, created to apprehend the world through play.[16] More important, toys are the materialization of play, the things that make play and are made for play. Toys are the matter of play.

It is important to characterize toys as technologies for or of play so we can describe the design of the objects in relation to their function in the ecology of play. Since toys are technologies, and technologies are instrumental in the ways the world is experienced, toys are also instrumental in the way they allow play to be experienced. Besides their cultural and emotional role, toys play an experiential role. Therefore, we need to look at their materiality in order to understand how they mediate play.

Before I propose a more formal analysis of what toys are, I have to admit that I am fascinated by the completeness of procedural toys and how they operate as alterity machines. Procedural toys are mesmerizing because they are frames of the otherness, because they are tiny worlds that operate by their own condition. However, despite this fascination, I prefer toys that present themselves as less open, less complete worlds.[17] The way Lego is an undone universe, or a universe yet to be invoked, is more enticing to me than playful simulating systems like *Sim City*. My views are biased, but knowingly so.

Culturally, a toy has been traditionally understood as a miniature, a model that allows a focused activity.[18] However, modern toys, particularly those running on computing devices, break the concept of the miniature and make us rethink toys from the perspective of objects that foster the characteristics of play. *Noby Noby Boy* illustrates how a toy takes over the functionality of a device, making it into a tool for play. We must think of the toy not as a miniature of a world but as a tool for play.[19]

The ecology of play is constituted by the elements that form the context of play: all the agents, situations, spaces, times, and technologies involved in playing. In this environment, toys play the role of props, of semiformalized embodiments of elements of the play activity. A ball is an embodiment of certain sports rules, coupled with a basic design around the essential pleasure of having only partial control over the movement of a physical object. We like balls because they allow us to score goals, but also because they are difficult to master. Balls are materials for play.

As props, toys are designed with certain affinities for some characteristics of play. Some toys are more fit for understanding the appropriative nature of play, while others reinforce the auto-telic, the expressive, or the personal.[20] *Noby Noby Boy* explores appropriation, and teddy bears explore expression. Toys are designed focused on the characteristics of play they are going to embody.

In this sense, toys have different dimensions.[21] These dimensions are the toy's physical manifestations of the characteristics of play, and they allow both designers and thinkers to better perceive and understand how play interacts with playthings and how play is incorporated into technologies and practices.

It is useful to divide these dimensions of play in two: filtering dimensions and manifestation dimensions. Don't look at the terminology as off-putting: I am writing about how toys embody the activity of play, how their materiality is related to the activity of play through their design.

The filtering dimensions are the designed functions that allow a toy to filter the elements of a play context in order to focus the activity it mediates. By filtering the context, toys suggest and afford certain manifestations of the play activity, as certain expressions that are enhanced by the use of the toy. The toy filters the context, focuses it, and makes it explicit. Through the toy, play is concretely formed, and it assumes a material form.[22]

There are only so many things one can do with the most basic of all toys, a ball. It can be bounced, rolled, and thrown, but not much else. The space and the activity around it are filtered through what the object can do best. We can playfully appropriate the toy, but it won't take us far. Similarly, Brian Eno and Peter Chilver's music toy *Bloom,* while behaving as an impressive generative music instrument, still filters the activity to provide a particular type of musical interaction, one based on timing between inputs, on rhythm rather than pitch or tonality.[23] When players touch any location on the screen, their input is translated into a repeating, clear sound that fades and returns. After several touches, the piece becomes an improvised music creation that we explore by touching it, with curiosity.

The filtering dimension of toys is focused on functionality, on how the toy adjusts to the different behaviors and actions that take place during play. In this sense, the filtering dimension of toys has nothing to do with their material constitution: a ball's filtering dimension is essentially the same regardless of whether it is a cloth, leather, or synthetic ball.

When we think about the filtering dimensions of toys, we face the question of how toys incorporate themselves in the activity of play. In classic design terms, we would be looking at the designed signifiers, affordances, and constraints. However, the idea of filtering allows greater flexibility, since it is not part of a conscious and methodological design process.[24] Making a toy requires understanding a play situation and creating an object for it, a process that can be performed by a professional designer but also by a child. The idea of filtering appeals to the openness of toy creation, that is, to everybody's capacity to create a toy.

The manifestation dimensions are more closely rooted in the material world. As I have noted, toys play a fundamental role in our sentimental life. They can embody times past, of childhood, and also of times when we played with others. The materiality of toys is important to understand how the object is experienced and what type of relations they establish with the context of play. Materiality is an important element for understanding affection and emotion.

Materiality matters when thinking about how toys act in a play context. From computer toys to self-made objects, from the sensual pleasures of wooden pieces to the touch-and-go immediacy of improvised parts scrambled together in a rush, the physicality of toys needs to be accounted for in order to understand the experience of play.

The manifestation dimensions of a toy focus on its physical materiality: the material it is made of, its technical platform, how it feels when we grasp it, how it becomes part of our memory. Toys are embodiments of play, and that embodiment can be analyzed by looking at the manifestation dimensions. It's not the same to play with a leather ball as it is with a synthetic one,[25] and it's not the same to interact with a software toy on a mobile platform as it is on a computer.

Vectorpark's *Levers* affords a different type of material experience when played on a computer (the touch pad mediation makes it a more distant affair for me) than on a mobile device (where the toy becomes a tactile experience).[26] *Levers* is a balancing toy that challenges its users to hang different things on the screen on levers, from whales to smoking pipes, trying to find a surreal balance over the sea. The toy is carefully designed around a physics simulation, and the tactile experience of hanging things on a lever to try to reach equilibrium is both intellectually satisfying and bodily pleasurable. Materiality matters in toys and play.

Toys, being objects in the world, need to be understood and made accountable in their physical presence. They need to be analyzed and created with a certain degree of awareness of their physical form, the place they occupy in the world and the way in which they occupy that place. The way toys filter play is relevant for understanding their role in the play activity, what actions they encourage, and how they do so; they way toys are physically manifested is crucial for understanding the emotional and intellectual responses to the play activity.

In this quest for understanding the ecology of play, toys are fundamental to understanding the technological and physical elements that constitute the contexts of play. Though this is an activity through which we understand the world, it is also deeply rooted in physical and material instantiations, in objects that carry part of the meanings of the activity, that help it exist and take place, be shared and be communicated. Toys are the physical embodiments of an ideal activity, the material realization of the ideals of play.

Toys seduce us, anchoring us in time and space; they trigger emotional responses, play a role in memory and culture, and help us devise situations so that play can take place. My idea of play is that of an activity full of romantic potential.[27] Toys bring these ideals to the material world, to the world of things. They help us locate, touch, feel, express, and share the ideals of play. As technologies of play, toys are the physical presence of play in the world, the tokens of our playful affection. Toys are instruments for letting play loose in the world, making us players. Toys are the tools of play.

4 Playgrounds

The ship is sinking! Fast, let's run to the moai. We will find shelter there from the pirates ... but where are you? Around which corner? Ah! There you are, hiding in the open belly of the ship! That was a good scare! What now?

All of these things happened to my oldest son and me on the same day in Copenhagen.

On a playground.

Our adventure took place in a *legeplads* (a Danish word that literally means "a playground") in the East of the city on a warm autumn day.[1] On our way to a family event, we had stumbled on a fantastically dramatic playground, a festival of shapes and structures organized around a sinking ship (figure 4.1) and a big statue like the moai on Easter Island.

The work of Danish playground designers Monstrum is astounding.[2] Not only they are able to infuse their structures with personality and charisma, but they also provide a dramatic setting for play that adults and children can enjoy together. Monstrum produces brilliant iterations of adventure playgrounds.[3]

But this chapter is not going to focus on the history of playgrounds. I want to think about play and space using playgrounds as both concrete examples and metaphors that explain the relationship between play and designed spaces.

Figure 4.1
A ship sinks in a playground.

So far in this book, I have focused on defining play and play-fulness and how the activity and attitude can be cued by the design of playthings. But where do we play, and how are those spaces designed? I don't want to think about game worlds, virtual or not, or about sports arenas. Those are spaces created for play, yes, but I aim at a more abstract and open category—at a parent species of all the different iterations of spaces for play. I want to reflect on how play modifies and is modified in and by physical or virtual environments.

Playgrounds are the most appropriate metaphor for understanding the interrelationships between play and actual playgrounds, but also skate parks and parks taken over by skaters or parkour traceurs (the moniker used for practitioners of parkour, the popular sport that uses city architectures for athletic explorative running) and, of course, virtual environments.

To understand the relationship between space and play, we need to return to two of the main arguments of this book: play is appropriative, and play takes place in the context of things, cultures, and people, in time and in space. The first fundamental distinction that we need to make is that between play spaces and game spaces. A play space is a location specifically created to accommodate play but does not impose any particular type of play, set of activities, purpose, or goal or reward structure. Playgrounds are the most typical play spaces, though the presence of toys in, for example, a doctor's waiting room is an invitation for the child (and the parents) to appropriate that space through play, to turn it into a play space.

A game space is a space specifically designed for a game activity. The size, measure, props, and even location are all created with the purpose of staging games. A game space can be created with the purpose of satisfying just one game, like some football stadiums in Europe, or with the purpose of supporting a multiplicity of games, like the old Roman arenas. Of course, the fact that game spaces are designed for games does not prevent them from being turned into play spaces. Again, play spaces are created when a space is appropriated though play.

In the digital realm, we could talk about the absolute dominance of game spaces over play spaces, from *Doom* to *Medal of Honor*. Most virtual game worlds are created to support a particular game, and the craft of level design is focused on the design of game spaces. Play spaces, however, are also an important tradition in virtual worlds. "Sandbox" games in which players can more or less freely roam an expansive virtual environment, like *Grand Theft Auto* and *Fallout 3*, are both game spaces and play spaces, and these are not the only games to include both spaces. Software toys like *Sim City* and other procedural toys are also play spaces to a large extent—spaces of possibility created to explore with rules in order to see what happens. Play spaces in digital games are linked to emergent behavior on both the material side (how the system behaves) and the user side.

The relationship between space and play is marked by the tension between appropriation and resistance: how a space offers itself to be appropriated by play, but how that space resists some forms of play, specifically those not allowed for political, legal, moral, or cultural reasons. Play relates to space through the ways of appropriation and the constant dance between resistance and surrender.

Let's return to the Danish Monstrum playgrounds, which are spaces designed for children to appropriate. They signal paths, activities, challenges, and possibilities; one can crawl, jump, creep up, roll, and fall in ways that the space suggests but does not determine. The dramatic flare of these playgrounds also indicates ways in which they could be appropriated. A sinking ship and a moai immediately invoke a set for imagined adventures where older kids can play pirates. The structure of these constructions encourages the creation of games of capture the flag, hide-and-seek, and tag. Different geometries and locations of the structures on the playground suggest many kinds of potential interactions. Both the materiality of the playground and its aesthetic form are ways of resisting pure appropriation, used to cue behaviors and therefore experiences, through play. But of course, play can always overrule design and make a carefully designed space something totally different, though still a space for play.

If we look at how a playground is designed, we notice how play in space is often organized around props. In the case of the Monstrum playground, the ship, the moai, and the hanging ropes all build up toward a particular place, a particular sequence of activities that can be performed: jump from the boat to the moai, climb up, find the ropes, slide through them (figure 4.2). Vertigo, order, structure, and chaos: they all potentially reside in the way this playground is structured and are all potential outcomes of this space.

The way spaces are articulated for play is dependent on more than design or playful considerations. Strong norms, rules, and laws govern the use of public and private spaces, and play design must be done in accordance with them. The Monstrum playgrounds are certified as safe, so they are institutionally correct. In many cases, the trivialization of playground design—the overabundance of plastic-based, repetitive architectures built for safety rather than for play—which seems to have increased in the past several decades, is a result of protective laws rather than of misguided design.[4] And the interest today in implementing digital playgrounds[5] or computer-enhanced environments[6] for play also comes from the normative idea that play is more secure if it is more controlled.

There is an interesting bit of history to this effect that helps explain how spaces are designed for play. Monstrum playgrounds,

Figure 4.2
Moais to play with.

as well as many of the playgrounds I frequent in Copenhagen, are the latest iteration of a Danish invention, the adventure playground.[7] Originally called "junk playgrounds," these spaces were created by progressive Danish pedagogues who were interested in letting children express themselves through play by providing them with the tools to create their playground. That is, instead of giving them a slide and a tower, they gave the children saws and hammers and nails so they could build their own playgrounds.

The obvious dangers of this practice created an interesting ripple effect: all play in adventure playgrounds was supervised by an adult. In this way, safety was moderately ensured. But this also meant that the children's play was monitored and potentially interfered with.[8] This is not a tale of absolute child freedom but an illustration of the careful balance needed when letting children be exposed to the creative, and potentially destructive, capacities of play.

Adventure playgrounds were adopted in Britain after World War II thanks to the efforts of Lady Allen of Hurtwood. After observing the Danish experience with adventure playgrounds, she imported the concept with two purposes. First, she saw these playgrounds as a way to help children reintegrate through play in constructive society after the war by letting them enjoy a larger degree of freedom than that granted in Victorian playgrounds. Second, playgrounds served as urban renewal projects since most of them were created in the shelled craters of bombed cities.

Certainly the history of the adventure playground is fascinating on its own, but the reason I invoke it here lies closer to my own understanding of play. Adventure playgrounds help us understand how spaces can be designed for play through the use of props that help play take place within a bounded space while still remaining open to the creative, appropriative capacities of the activity. Good playgrounds open themselves up to play, and their props serve as instruments for playful occupation.[9]

The question of how to design these spaces is an architectural one.[10] We should worry about how a space is created for facilitating play while complying with the different normative frames in which play takes place. This is a challenge, since norms and regulations are often conservative estimates based on the types of play we deem correct,[11] and often those are based on fear rather than on the potential for play to be an expressive way of being in the world.

Playgrounds are interesting because they are spaces designed for appropriation. However, we should not underestimate the capacity of play to appropriate the world outside the environments we create for it. Think about urban sports, from skateboarding to parkour. Both sports play with space or, more appropriately, appropriate the space of the city in order to perform play activities.

Skateboarders are masters at seeing the playground in the urban spaces that surround them.[12] A rail is for play, and so are stairs. The more public and the more complicated the space, the better the play is. Some cities have built expensive skate parks, yet on weekend nights, you can find teenagers revealing to us how mundane our public environments are, for what we think is a square is just a reflection of our own view. To these young people, it's not a square; it's a playground, and it is theirs.

Similarly, parkour appropriates and reinterprets urban spaces, making the architecture of the city not only an obstacle but also an expressive instrument.[13] Although many cities are now building parkour playgrounds, it is the urban space where the traceurs find the most interesting routes to express themselves. The importance of recording and sharing the different feats is connected to the deeply embodied experience of the space that parkour promotes. Parkour is about the traceurs taking over an urban space together, making it a canvas for bodily expression

The next step in thinking about playgrounds comes from the digital domain. Computers have allowed us to create increasingly sophisticated virtual worlds. These worlds are mostly created for playing. One could argue, in fact, that one of the main contributions of computing to the history of games is the capacity to create complex, interactive worlds.[14]

It is not my intention to go deep into computer games in this book; after all, they are just a tiny subset of playthings. But I briefly reflect on how computers help create both game spaces and play spaces and why playgrounds are good metaphors to understand them.

I first focus on video games that offer an open world that is not structured exclusively around the form of a game but a world that contains a game, or many games. *Grand Theft Auto*, *Fallout 3*, and even most massively multiplayer online games are, to a certain extent, sandbox games. They are interesting because their design is the digital implementation of the idea of a space open for appropriation yet populated by props that help steer predetermined activities.

Think about *Grand Theft Auto:* although the game wants us to follow its linear, narrative structure, the storytelling nodes that move the plot forward are in fact props, like all the other things in that world for encouraging play. The narrative takes us into a game with form and structure, but we don't need to engage with it. We can take another route and see what happens, as we would on a playground.

Software toys share this nature. *Sim City* encourages players to develop the city, which provides interesting challenges and audiovisual positive feedback when the city becomes larger.[15] However, much of the joy in interacting with these procedural toys comes from testing their very *propness* as we figure out where the seams are and what we can build with them. They are somewhat like adventure playgrounds, giving us a hammer and some nails while a vigilant adult makes sure that we are never idle or that we use the hammer on our best friend's head.

A different take on the playground can be found in experimental games that use the computer's capacity to create virtual spaces to provide not a tempting dance between structured and unstructured play but a more contemplative experience. These are games on the limit of being playgrounds. They could be perhaps better understood as a concept between a playground that uses the conventional rhetoric of play and a romantic garden designed for suggesting potential but never actual activities. I call these *emotional playgrounds:* spaces designed for using the experience of play rather than its form to create emotions.

The video game *Proteus* (figure 4.3) is an example of this kind of emotional playground.[16] In *Proteus*, players are free to wander around a computer-generated island with birds and butterflies; stones and trees; snow and rain and sun; and seasons and stars. The *Proteus* player, accompanied by music, sets off to fulfill his or her goal of exploring a world.

Proteus is interactive software that delivers an experience to which we open ourselves; we cocreate an experience while engaging with that world in the mood of play. *Proteus* uses play to explore emotions—in my case, longing, the pleasure of solitude, and inner peace. Walking in *Proteus* is walking in a playground designed to explore not the props laid out and placed

Figure 4.3
Entering the world of *Proteus*.

there by the creator of the space to interact with but a playground designed for us to fill with our own emotional props, which can then be experienced through play.

Proteus is a way forward in digital world design. By harnessing the world-creating capacities of software but focusing on the emotional capacities of play, *Proteus* invites us to explore through play and allow ourselves to enter a state in which we become the subject of experience and inquiry. The beauty in *Proteus* comes from its openness to us to take it over and complete it.

Computers might have afforded a whole new way of understanding and creating playgrounds. The capacity of programmers to write their own physics and logic makes it possible to create worlds with different coherences from ours, that is, with different laws of physics, time, or even materiality. Digital playgrounds are still trying to formulate ways in which the important materiality of the props of material playgrounds can be substituted, to the same effect.

Playgrounds explain how materiality and activity are joined together in the selected spaces of play. Playgrounds as metaphors also allow us to escape from game spaces, which are designed for the purpose of playing games but do not always allow the exploration of the creative and appropriative capacities of play. If play spaces are defined by something, from skater parks to *Proteus*, that is the openness to appropriation, the ways in which they let us play, giving us a place to be.

5 Beauty

We have so far covered play as expression, through toys and in space, as an activity or an attitude. Now I focus on why play is not only important but also beautiful. Let's talk about beauty. And let's start by making things complicated: since I wrote *beauty*, let's talk art.[1] Is play an artistic manifestation? Are playthings, from toys to games, "art"? To be honest, and a bit of a tease, I don't care, so I will stay away from that discussion. The type of understanding of play I advocate is obviously "artistic": it is in the roots of a wide diversity of "works of art," from Rabelais and Cervantes[2] to Yoko Ono and John Cage.[3] From medieval theater and festivals to Fluxus and performance art,[4] play and playfulness have often been a strategy to either produce works of art or challenge the art world establishment, bringing a change of paradigm to "the arts."[5]

But "the arts" don't interest me. I am interested in how some instances of play, some acts of performing playful actions, lead to aesthetic beauty—to an experience that not only becomes memorable but also proposes a new way of seeing the world. I am interested in the beauty of play.[6]

There have already been many reflections on the close relationship between play and aesthetics.[7] Most thinkers seem to conclude that if there is an aesthetics of play, it happens in the intersection of the activity of the players with the formal elements of the game.[8] Beauty happens in play, understood as that transitional activity between the different nodes of the play environment, between the things and the players and the context and cultures. The act of appropriating the form of play and doing something unusual or unexpected is beautiful; it is also beautiful to perfect the mechanized interaction between human and system. That is the aesthetics of play I am interested in exploring.

This is, of course, *one* aesthetic of play. If we understand aesthetics as the philosophical investigation on beauty, then it is possible to accept a multiplicity of valid ways of understanding the aesthetics of play. Other aesthetics of play might be focused on the forms of play, either as mass-produced objects of consumption that are cultural hybrids or as procedural machines that excel at simulating processes.[9]

Mine is a nonformalist aesthetics of play, inspired by contemporary art theories, like Bourriaud's relational aesthetics,[10] Kester's conversational aesthetics[11] as filtered though Bishop's critiques,[12] and Kaprow's writings on performance art.[13] Each of them illustrates different aspects that together will help me sketch an aesthetic theory of play.

I start from the beginning: Why is play beautiful? Seeing the performance of a top athlete—a runner or a football player or a StarCraft maestro—fills our senses with a bodily admiration, with a perception of truth that makes it worth contemplating their actions.[14] Play is full of instances of beauty—both observed play and experienced play that give us a way of seeing the world through the eyes of beauty.[15]

The beauty of play might take its origins in the form of play. The formal elegance of the rules of Go or the size of a soccer field lead to a rational understanding of how interesting it is to perform actions within those boundaries. The beauty of the offside rule in soccer or the spawn locations in *Modern Warfare 2* are also formal examples of how playthings can be beautiful in the way they constrain actions and facilitate expression through play. The offside rule forces offensive soccer players to constantly perform a dancelike interaction with the defenders, creating an imaginary line that can be overcome by the (beautiful) combination of physical and mental prowess. In those dances with failure lies the beauty of the constrained performances we call sports.

But there is more to play than its form. We can think about the beauty of winning, as in runaway victories or in dramatic, last-moment changes of scores that propel unexpected results. The last-minute goal, the gravity-defying three-pointer, the comeback surge of units in the last stage of the game: these suggest the beauty of winning.[16] But there is more to play than the scores and the results, that is, the statistics of play.

Let's look in a different direction, away from the action of play as framed by a thing or a system that can be won. I propose an aesthetics of play as action or, better put, the aesthetics of play as the action of appropriation and expression of and within a context.[17]

Although the world of sports offers a relatively easy approach to illustrate this understanding of aesthetics through play, I start by pointing to a computer game as a source of beauty. The computer game *GIRP* is a rock-climbing simulator in which each rock the player can grip has a key assigned to it. Players must use a special key to "flex" while simultaneously pressing the key assigned to the rock they are gripping and the rock they want to grip. *GIRP* is an exercise in reflective masochism, a constant fight with the physical layout of the keyboard and the limits of our own hand flexibility. That is the source of beauty: the painful and abusive input system mimics the very act of rock climbing and its difficulty and teases us to continue playing despite the pain and hardship it puts us through.

In 2011, *GIRP* was remixed into *Mega-GIRP,* an installation game in which the keys were distributed over dance mat controllers (mats with buttons to step or dance on) laid down on the floor.[18] The challenge now was more physical, highlighting an element of beauty partially hidden in the browser version of *GIRP*: the pleasure of finding not only an appropriate route but one that was also physically pleasurable. Musicians know there is a certain tactile pleasure in playing an instrument in some specific ways. Similarly, *GIRP* players sometimes prefer routes that have a rhythm, a certain beauty in the move between keys. *Mega-GIRP* made the game more physically beautiful, a more engaging spectacle to see, a more transparent aesthetic work.

This is the first way in which we can connect this aesthetics of play with contemporary art. In this understanding of play, the objects, while important, are only part of a context of play.[19] In contemporary art theory, relational aesthetics somewhat evokes this similarity with play. Relational aesthetics refers to works of art that in the mid- to late 1990s challenged the traditional focus on the art object as a thing.[20] Relational aesthetics describes the aesthetic and artistic value of works focused on creating particular social contexts that create specific human relations.[21]

One of the most famous pieces of relational aesthetics is Rirkrit Tiravanija's installation *Untitled (Free/Still)* (1992), in which the artist cooked food for visitors at a gallery.[22] The aesthetics of this piece, Bourriaud (2002) claims, comes not from the piece itself or even the context in which it takes place, but from the way in which the piece creates a space for awareness and discussion of topics such as refugees and their social conditions. Relational aesthetics encompasses work in which the artist creates a space for human relations in a particular context and through a specific activity.

It seems obvious that some instances of play can be described as relational aesthetics. A game like *Flingle* for the iPad, with its subtle cues for flirting and sexual innuendo, creates instances of beauty through its capacity to appropriate the context of play and establish the possibility of flirting.[23] *Flingle* is a puzzle game for two players designed to make the players touch each other's hands. It's a game about gestures, about the subtle (and not-so-subtle) play with hands that might happen during flirting. In this sense, the game becomes a secondary affair, since the context and the relations between players are pushed into the foreground. *Flingle*, like other modern party games, appropriates social contexts, only to vanish in the background, eliciting an excuse for unleashing play in interesting ways within that context.

Many folk games can be seen as examples of relational aesthetics. Ninja, for example, is beautiful when it is played in a public space, disrupting other people's daily lives and creating a different environment by playful appropriation of that space.[24] Similarly, playful technologies, by disrupting the normal flow of interaction, can act as an opening for conversations within a context. A playful technology can allow a material-based critique of a context by highlighting its own existence through play. What we can do unwillingly or what we take for granted can be revealed playfully, and so a space for conversation is created.

Moritz Greiner-Petter's Precise Ambiguity project illustrates how a subtle change in the design of an object changes the context of interaction and its meaning.[25] The piece called *TICK* adds arbitrary curls to the mouse cursor on screen, initially annoying the user but then allowing for a short interruption of play in the process of productivity. That opening is where a dialogue might happen and also the space of the aesthetics of play.

Relational aesthetics, however, poses deep problems.[26] The importance of the artist and the space (usually the gallery) may lead to questions about the way in which the communities are created. It is true that relational aesthetics creates relations between people in a context, but the context and the relations are inevitably determined by the nature of the predetermined space and the awareness of the artist as creator and the audience as complicit.

In the case of play and games, this might not be an issue. Play can happen everywhere and anywhere, and it can happen by appropriating any space. Relational aesthetics falls short in describing what kind of experiences the art piece creates, and it particularly fails at addressing how art can be a radical experiment in aesthetics and social change.[27] What we need is an aesthetic theory that focuses on community creation through values and ideals—a theory that connects expression with context and the piece of art. Grant Kester's dialogical aesthetics can be used to understand cases in which play happens as a catalyst of communities of values or of ideas.[28]

Dialogical aesthetics focuses on the concept of dialogue in a context rather than an art piece situated in a context.[29] It is not only that the context is important, but also how the work of art inserts itself in a situation in order to facilitate a dialogue. Aesthetics has always brought new knowledge to the world or new ways of seeing the world. In classic aesthetics, the objects were charged with this task. In dialogical aesthetics, artistic practice voluntarily tackles the creation of new knowledge not though an object but through the emergence of a context in which dialogue and conversation are suddenly possible or allowed.[30] The aesthetic experience happens in the dialogue not only in the uttering, but also in the act of listening, in the spaces open for expression and reception of ideas.

A case of dialogical aesthetics can be found in abusive games or games that explore the seams between actions and beings in play and outside play.[31] Nordic live action role playing games,[32] and particularly the experimental type of Jeepen games,[33] explore extremely thorny issues through play. In Fat Man Down, players have to role-play the bullying of the fattest player.[34] This is not the player role-playing a fat person—the actual player with more actual body fat. While the game might be played for fun, its correlation with actions that are not within the play activity opens up what has been called *bleed* for the transmission of experiences and knowledge from the activity of play to our worldview.[35] Jeepen games use play to appropriate a context and a community, opening them up to a dialogic extreme experience. In that context, the aesthetic facilitated by play takes place.

Dialogical aesthetics downplays the importance of the object in favor of the dialogue that emerges among participants. The plaything, even as initiator of the situation, is not important because the aesthetic experience takes place in the dialogue among participants, context, creator, and culture. Aesthetics happen in the context, through the action, and that is why play and dialogical aesthetics are well matched; play too is a contextual appropriation of a situation with the purpose of creating new values, expressions, or knowledge.

In this sense, the aesthetics of play is close to the aesthetics of performances, particularly of Kaprow's understandings of art.

Kaprow (2003) summarizes a long tradition of using play as an element of artistic practice. From Dada and surrealism to Fluxus and situationism, the history of art in the twentieth century is that of a playful appropriation and demolishing of conventions that were elevated by the modernist movement of the late nineteenth century. Through play, situationists, surrealists, Dada, and Fluxus artists subverted any possible establishment, using games and toys as manifestations of their aesthetic ideals.

Following this tradition, Kaprow (2003) describes play as a force behind the happenings,[36] that is, a way of engaging against the formalisms of "art"[37] and a way of exploring what can be done with art. For Kaprow, play is a force on its own—a dirty word that breaks the world and collapses social arrangements and makes things happen. The ideals behind Kaprow's play are those of participation and humor, and an experiment in which boundaries can be broken by merely acting through play.

Abusive games like *Desert Bus* are Kaprowian games, using play to bomb the conventions of play from within, forcing us to rethink our compulsion to keep on playing even though we know that the goals are meaningless and the action is trivial.[38] *Desert Bus* is a game that commands players to drive a bus from Tucson to Las Vegas at a maximum speed of 45 mph. Since the distance computer in the program is accurate, this is a trip done in real time. The trip takes eight hours, in which the game cannot be stopped. Furthermore, the bus steers slightly to the right, which forces players to provide constant input. A player who reaches Las Vegas is awarded one point.

In *Desert Bus*, there is no proper winning or losing, and the act of playing is so excruciatingly boring that it reveals the act of playing in itself as something to reflect on. *Desert Bus*, like all other abusive games, is a game against games; it uses play to appropriate the conventions of the form of games and turns them around, marginalizing the importance of the object in favor of the activity of playing. Playing *Desert Bus* means coming to the realization that play cannot be constrained to results, that it must happen toward a performative, expressive purpose. *Desert Bus* merges art and life in the eight-hour bus trip to Las Vegas.

One way in which play can be aesthetically interesting happens when the need to keep playing is combined with a game that resists the pleasures and comforts of playing in order to push particular painful behaviors, like the impossible struggle to win a game not meant to be won in *Desert Bus*.[39] Instead of a game that wants to give pleasure to players and help them play, abusive game designs make the user willing to play a "dirty" act that requires submission to an unfriendly situation, to games we want to play but that refuse to be played.[40] Playing *Desert Bus* is a "dirty" act inasmuch as it requires submission to an absurd game design that refuses to ease the act of playing. Through that abuse, aesthetic experiences take place:[41] not *thanks to* the object, not *through* the object, but in the act of playing with it, and making sense of our own activity as we struggle to play with them.

There are many forms of seeing the aesthetics of play. I have presented three different understandings of the beauty of play that are deeply rooted in contemporary art theories and in accordance with the appropriative, creative nature of play. These are nonformalist views on the aesthetics of play—understandings of beauty that are not dependent on an object, but on behaviors, attitudes, and activities that take into consideration objects, people, contexts, and cultures. While this might not be the most appropriate way for understanding the aesthetics of some games and toys, and the practices derived from them,[42] any aesthetic understanding of play needs to see it as a performance in which form becomes secondary to the activity itself. Besides an aesthetics of playthings, I advocate for play as an aesthetic practice.[43]

An aesthetics of play needs to be rooted in the performance of play, that is, in what happens when play takes over and becomes the dominant mode of being in the world. This means looking at the contexts and modes of production of that performance, from improvised play in the corners of a city to the mass-organized contemporary sports events. The ways in which we produce and consume play are also crucial in understanding play as an aesthetic practice. The aesthetics of play performance are dependent on the contextual and material situations in which performance takes place.

When thinking about play, we might risk forgetting the importance of the playthings, the time, the culture, and all the other elements of the ecological environment of the play activity. When I refer to play as an aesthetic practice, I don't want to limit the perspective to the performance; rather, I look at the extended activity. The activity is the most important thing to look at—the starting point for play as aesthetic practice. However, the materiality of playthings, the situations and contexts, the people and the purpose that surround the activity: they all play a role. When they all come together, in whatever form of dissonance or accord that makes us understand the world in a new way or see things that were invisible to us, then play becomes aesthesis, and beauty takes over, occupying through play our being in the world.

6 Politics

Tommie Smith. Jesse Owens. Diego Armando Maradona. Martina Navratilova. All of these athletes transcended their role as players, giving their performances a political meaning, whether voluntarily, like Smith, or involuntarily, like Maradona.[1]

Let's look at Maradona's historical peak, the second goal against England in the 1986 Soccer World Cup in Mexico.[2] In what has been described as the goal of the century, Maradona took the ball in the midfield and dashed across the pitch, dribbling half of the English team until he scored. This Argentinian from the slums humiliated England as England had humiliated Argentina in the Falklands.[3]

I am of course reading politics into a soccer goal. But in our world of global spectacles, play through sports has gained unparalleled political influence. In our modern understanding of play, these activities have defining and identifying roles in society. Even critical thinkers like Adorno thought that sports were a key source of alienation,[4] granting social and political importance to play.[5] But why do we correlate play and politics so often?

Let's start with play itself. Two of the key characteristics of play are its appropriative nature and the creativity that ensues. Play is creative when it is taking over, or occupying, a context.

Similarly, the playful attitude takes over an activity in a creative manner, even though its purpose remains unchanged. Appropriation leads to carnivalesque creativity, which might lead to a critical approach to the context, the very act of play, or the activity that is being playfully occupied. It is therefore natural to think that play can be used for political purposes, instrumentalized to become a tool for expressing political ideas.

This understanding of the critical nature of play has been widely explored. The notion of critical politics through play has a long standing in Latin America,[6] where it has been coupled with a Marxist understanding of the individual and his or her relation to power and the means of production.[7] For thinkers like Augusto Boal and Paulo Freire, play is a critical liberating force that can be used to explore the ultimate possibility of human freedom[8]. Similarly, Nordic live action role playing games (LARPs)[9] have played with dystopian scenarios[10] and more political situations[11] in ways that no other game has explored. From building a makeshift concentration camp to proposing a game about the final hours of civilization in the 1950s, LARPs have dealt with the politics of the state as well as with individual politics, using play to explore political meaning.

In the context of political arts, play has had an immense influence: Guy Debord's situationism[12] and its contemporary presence through *Adbusters*, a Canadian anticonsumerist magazine;[13] Dada's anarchism,[14] initially targeted at the art world but soon expanding to society in general; and Fluxus's humorous and mildly naive[15] understanding of political expression: all show how aesthetics has approached politics through play thanks to the appropriative nature of play.

In contemporary times, political games seem to signify things other than these creative, communitarian activities of expression. The expression "political computer games" seems to mean single-player computer games developed for the PC using widespread platforms like Flash, in which the topic is political and the game play is a rehash of old and trite gaming common places, from *Space Invaders* to *Tetris* mechanics camouflaged under a skin of political themes.[16] The "political" game is just a (single) player game that addresses a political theme of the moment and then rapidly vanishes from the public scene.

In fact, the most important critique that one could leverage against the trend of political game play championed in modern game design concerns the way it ignores that it is in play, and not in games, where politics resides. Like any other object or instrument or technology, games are political, but the true political effect of these objects takes place when we occupy them, that is, when they become instruments for political expression. The game or toy is only a rhetorical argument—political expression at most, if not propaganda. Politics happens when play becomes political action.[17]

To play is to exercise our being as expressive creatures, including as political creatures. We express politics in many ways: through voting and love, through writing and labor, through service and values, and also through play.

Games can be political. (Dishwashers can be political too: how much electricity does yours use?) But when play is political, it happens in a critical, personal, creative way. Some modern political games are not played; we perform operations in order to activate and configure their messages. That is hardly a creative, appropriative activity. In fact, it is a guided activity through power structures toward purposes dictated beforehand. Playing these games is not about affirming but about reaffirming.

Political play takes place when a plaything harnesses the expressive, creative, appropriative, and subversive capacities of play and uses them for political expression. Political play is the interplay of form, appropriation, and context, or how politics is expressed and enacted through play in a fluid motion.

To see this theory in practice, consider the popular protests that took over the world between 2009 and 2012, from the Arab Spring to the Occupy movement. Revolts and demonstrations are political expressions that the established powers often meet with fear, which often leads to police action. In the protests of late 2009 and 2010 that took place across the United Kingdom, a police tactic for containing dissenters became popular: kettling.[18] Kettling consists of surrounding a group of protesters with enough riot police to contain them in an area, either to facilitate their arrest or to break down large demonstrations into more manageable groups. Kettling is not necessarily a violent tactic, but it immediately showcases the force of riot police. Kettling is also the inspiration for one of the most interesting political games ever made: Metakettle.[19]

The rules of Metakettle are simple:

1. Shout "Metakettle" to start the game.
2. Start your own team by shouting an animal name or join an already established team by linking arms with them.
3. Get other people on your team by completely encircling them with members of your team.
4. The person who formed the last surviving animal team wins.
5. Repeat until the police let you go.

It makes sense to play Metakettle only when being kettled. Metakettle is designed to appropriate a particular situation and playfully turn it around. It is carnivalesque play at its best—an appropriation of a situation turned into the absurd through play that shows a political interpretation of the situation in which it is played.

From a formal point of view, we might be tempted to argue that the rules of the game make it political. However, Metakettle is political only if played when kettled. Playing it in other situations is almost identity shopping, because Metakettle requires a context to be a political statement: it is a playful bomb designed to go off through laughter in play. We can appreciate its cleverness and can write about it as a political device, but its political effect, the expression of political action through play, happens only when Metakettle is played while being kettled. Then, and only then, does play become a carnivalesque, disruptive, political mode of being.

Political action through play is also benefiting from the paradoxical nature of play. Since play is autotelic, one could argue that the purpose of playing Metakettle is "to play Metakettle," which is not a political activity. However, it is precisely the autotelic nature of play that makes it political action. Like carnival, play has a particular status in its relation to reality that allows political action while being relatively immune to the actions of power. Shutting down a game of Metakettle will only reinforce the message of playing it as political action. In this way, once you start playing Metakettle, the police have already lost—the game *and* their moral ground. Play as political action can either be shut down with extreme force or be ignored, and in both cases the political purpose of play will be made evident.

The humor in Metakettle relates this type of political play to art practices like Fluxus and situationism,[20] which made use of humorous play to promote political views and ideas.[21] Although these movements share the focus on playful humor, they are still focused on an artist-to-audience communication model.[22] Performance art is closer to the spirit of political action through play,[23] even though political play is a communitarian activity that is not necessarily guided. Political meaning emerges from the play community and from the ways in which play threads together context, form, and situation.

The hacktivist group Anonymous provides another example of political play; this one is less dependent on games and more focused on rules emerging from the community.[24] The history of Anonymous is quite complex.[25] It was born on the Internet image board 4chan, a site where all kinds of images, from innocent to borderline illegal, are uploaded by users who remain anonymous.[26] The culture of lulz, the surreal, Dada, offensive, and childish humor based on image manipulation and silly captions,[27] thrived on these boards. Then it took a political direction. A group of 4chaners took on the challenge of defying the Church of Scientology.[28] And from that initial challenge, a worldwide group of protesters took to the streets as an activist group in a wide variety of topics.[29]

What makes the Anonymous take on the Church of Scientology interesting is the transportation of Internet anonymity and activism to real-life anonymity and activism. The move from the Internet to real life preserved some of the core political values of the Net, like anonymity, making the actual number of activists difficult to quantify. And in a corresponding move, they took to the real-world Internet memes and jokes, occupying the physical world with expression that previously existed only on the Internet. In London, the headquarters of the Church of Scientology was rickrolled—that is, forced to listen for hours to loudspeakers playing Rick Astley's hit "Never Gonna Give You Up."[30]

Anonymous performs political play precisely because the group imported Internet memes to the physical world, creating a carnivalesque protest in between worlds. It performs political action without eliminating its roots on Internet culture and plays because it appropriates the real world through the rhetoric of Internet memes and lulz. The protesters express political ideas, but they are also playing, performing specific actions with specific meanings within their own community. It's play closer to performance art than to games.[31] The Internet memes brought to life are negotiable toys that frame and situate play. Without them, Anonymous would not be playing: protesting, yes, but not playing.

An example of the attitude of playfulness is the reappropriation of unpleasant designs, as described by artists Gordan Savicic and Selena Savic.[32] "Unpleasant design" describes the use of industrial or interaction design to make certain "undesired" activities, like skating in a public park, difficult or impossible. But these designs can be subverted by playful political appropriation. For instance, Michael Rakowitz's ParaSITE creates inflatable shelters that reuse the warm air from heat exchangers.[33] This playful political and social statement not only reclaims the public space, but also highlights resource wastefulness and the situation of the homeless in cities.

Not every political action through play, or playfulness, requires this loose approach to rules, this negotiation of frame and context. In fact, it is still possible to find political action through play and playfulness incorporated in the processes of computer systems. There are technologies for play and playfulness that insert themselves in a context to perform political actions.

An approach to the political nature of technologies is critical engineering.[34] One of its products, Newstweek, is a paradigmatic example of political playfulness.[35] Newstweek is a critical intervention on the digital consumption of news and the nature of networks as carriers of messages and information. It is a small hardware/software combination designed to interfere with open wireless networks (figure 6.1). In these networks, the device modifies the headlines of popular news websites, disfiguring the relative trust we place in the neutrality of networks and network communication.

Newstweek is not a device that creates play or a toy, but its approach to public spaces, networks, and news sites is certainly playful. It literally appropriates a context and situation and

Figure 6.1
The Newstweek device. (Credit: Julian Oliver and Danja Vasiliev.)

makes it playful. That appropriation is a political action that reveals assumptions and beliefs through which we articulate our daily life. Newstweek critiques computer and news networks, their linkage, and the ways we trust them.

Newstweek is also a carnivalesque project, intervening in the public sphere to make arguments through playfulness and technology. It is a public critique of power, a multilayered satire that operates superficially on the rendered website pages, but more deeply on the computer networks that it critiques and mocks (figure 6.2). Newstweek's open source nature adds to this carnivalesque humor: anybody can build and deploy a Newstweek. It is an open, public, inclusive engagement device through critical technologies that embody the freedom of playfulness.

Figure 6.2
"Promotional" picture for the Newstweek news manipulation device. (Image credit: Julian Oliver and Danja Vasiliev.)

Newstweek is an act of appropriation of a public context with the intention of promoting political action. This appropriation is playful, demanding from knowledgeable appreciators a certain sense of humor. It playfully forces us to rethink our position as consumers and producers of news through computer networks, and it comments as well on the assumptions on trust and neutrality that we place on wireless connections. Through Newstweek, we appropriate political assumptions and critically reflect on them.

Play is political, then, not because the playthings or the contexts in which we play are openly political, either rhetorically or socially. Neither is play political because it is constituted of actions that can be interpreted as socially conscious or activist. Play is political in the way it critically engages with a context, appropriating it and using the autotelic nature of play to turn actions into double-edged meanings: they are actions both in a play activity and with political meaning and are therefore are heavy with meaning.

Play has the capacity to remain play while giving the actions performed political meaning, from dribbling Englishmen in a football pitch to metakettling protesters already kettled by riot police. It is no wonder that play as political action is so close to critical theater: it shares the ambiguous nature of an activity that can move between boundaries and meanings, as an act with its own purpose and as direct political action, seamlessly interwoven.

Political play takes place when the focus of the play activity is set on the appropriative nature of play and how that appropriation can be used creatively to subvert the establishment, institutions, or other forces. Play becomes political action when the interplay between the context and the appropriation lead to an activity that critically engages with the situation without ceasing to be play.

Play as political action is always ambiguous, on the fence of autotelic play and meaningful political activity. It is in that interplay, in that dance between the autotelic and the purposeful, that play becomes a strong political instrument, capable of appropriating contexts that are otherwise forbidden. Political play is expression of political ideas in the seams opened by appropriation; it is a critical expression through playful interpretation of a context. Because it is play, it can thrive in situations of oppression; because it is play, it can allow personal and collective expression, giving voices and actions when no one can be heard.

7 Architects

Sometimes the beauty of play resides in the tension between control and chaos. Sometimes playing is voluntarily surrendering to form; sometimes it is being seduced into form, being appropriated by a plaything. Some other times, the pleasure comes from the appropriation of those forms, breaking and deforming them to play with them.

By "the form of play" I am referring to games more than to toys, which tend to be freer and less formal.[1] To these artifacts we surrender ourselves to being seduced. Form implies that it can be communicated, transmitted, fixed and polished, and adapted and modified.[2] The form of football is kept under vigilance by the Fédération Internationale de Football Association (FIFA) and UEFA,[3] the form of basketball by the National Basketball Association and the International Basketball Association. Despite the myriad house rules and interpretations of Scrabble, when professional games take place, there is a shared set of rules that account for what competitive Scrabble should be.[4] Form is the common language that allows us to share a game—and to design it.

Form also allows us to be seduced, with the seduction starting the process of play. Form gives us a starting point. Play has to begin somewhere, and it does so by occupying a context with its form, typically the rules of a game. When a referee in any sport signals the beginning of the game, the world changes, and in that space, players and spectators experience a new reality. Similarly, when a computer game begins, a new loop in the program starts, virtually taking over the machine and its resources. Through form, appropriation begins; it is the starting point from which play plays itself.[5]

Because play happens through form and is a way of being in the world, the cultural capital of the act of creating the form of play has dramatically increased.[6] From interaction design to performance art and game design, the activity of creating play, or invoking playfulness, is slowly becoming intellectual work. The form of play obsesses our culture. Of course, this is the wrong obsession, since what is important about play is not its form, which will, after all, mutate as part of play itself, but the activity or the attitude, that is, the process of engaging with the world and oneself through play.

Games are, to a certain extent, a privileged form of play. Games are *the* culture-dominant material manifestation of the autotelic nature of play.[7] Performances and rituals have religious or aesthetic purposes, while games are just games, serving a purpose of their own. To understand play, we often focus on games. In this ecological approach to play, which levels the activity and the related attitude across technologies and contexts, I see no preference in the understanding of play. Games are just another manifestation of play.

However, games have also gained enormous cultural capital since the beginning of this century.[8] The success of computer games overshadows many other developments,[9] but the presence in our culture of many types of games, from sports to board games and even reality TV contests, is a testimony to the importance of play in our culture. This surge in the interest in games and the dominance of digital games in our leisure economy have contributed to the rise in cultural capital of games as a form of play.

Many academics and game designers have argued that games will be the dominant aesthetic form of this century, taking over the central cultural position of movies, television, and literature. This is an interesting argument for those of us interested in play, since games are just a formal manifestation of play. But one of the consequences of this argument is deeply interesting: the rise in importance of game design as a practice, and therefore the role of the creator of games in our culture of leisure.

Play is a powerful manifestation of knowledge and being in the world, a way of becoming, learning, and expressing ourselves that is deeply and inherently human, though never isolated from a world of cultures and materials with which we play, they themselves playing too. And since games are the privileged way of channeling play through form, making games must be an important social activity. Besides the academic and commercial interest in game design, there is also a cultural interest in vindicating the role of the creator of games as an important member of the culture industries.

There are many reasons behind this vindication, but the one I consider most important has to do with our rationalist, post-Enlightenment, postromantic societies and the privilege we give to those able of creating and understanding both mechanical creation and human expression.[10] The game designer is a figure who understands how humans enjoy playing, mastering the necessary materials that lead to successful play. This designer is a romantic author, a creator who knows about what we access only through intuition and can materially create those experiences.

The art of game design is the art of creating play. This enlightened attribute of the designer—the capacity to harness, control, steer and produce play for intended purposes—is what makes them culturally respectable.

However, this idea of game design does not always match with play being a creative force, a sometimes dangerous, sometimes excessive form of being and expression that belongs to the person who chooses to play. Play is appropriation, and therefore its relations with form are complicated. Form encapsulates, shapes, and steers play to a certain extent, but it is also seduced by play and appropriated by it. Within this idea of play, what is game design? How can these privileged forms of play be created?

Before I answer this question, I quickly summarize the modern understanding of game design as a practice and how it relates to play. In this context of increasing cultural capital conceded to games and play, game design has become one of the fastest-growing areas of the discipline of design in terms of recognition.[11]

A central discourse in game design writing focuses on the relation between games and system design. This way of thinking focuses on crafting systems that involve players and express ideas.[12] Games are seen as expressive objects thanks to their formal design, since they convey meaning through systems. Game designers write about and focus on the form of games as being systems that encapsulate, coordinate, frame, and to a certain extent determine play.

Meaning is then embedded in systems, and players are given the role of relatively creative beings who interact with the system in order to find meaning in the form. Through the system, and not through appropriation, formal play through games becomes a way of knowledge.

I disagree with this view of game design. I don't disagree with the notion that games are, for the most part, systems, and that is why computers have contributed to their cultural importance. However, system-centric design thinking—the idea that because games are systems, they are important—is contrary to the way these systems are experienced. Game systems can only partially contain meaning, because meaning is created through an activity that is contextual, appropriative, creative, disruptive, and deeply personal. Games are props for that activity; they are important because they focus on it, not because they contain or trigger its meaning. Games are important because they are the privileged form of play, but they are only a form of play.

In order to understand how we can rethink how games are created and how that process can be adapted to the nature of play, we need to look back at design theory and research to understand what the nature of design is and how it matches the nature of play.

So what is design? This apparently simple question has been asked in design research for decades,[13] and it is by no means my intention to engage in that conversation. So I will keep it simple: design is the science of the artificial, a discipline focused on creating new technological objects in the world for specific uses. It is concerned with the creation of new things in the world. Design is also a mode of knowledge:[14] if the natural sciences understand the natural world and the humanities and social sciences try to explain people, design is posed to understand the artificial—or, more precisely, the way the materiality of the artificial interfaces with the world. Designers must know about materiality; they must be familiar with how materials can be bent and manipulated to a purpose. But a designer must also know people: how they interact with objects, how they relate to the future state of affairs encapsulated in a designed object, and how they feel.

To design is to know how materials can be translated into objects that will please, enhance, satisfy, and even create needs. To design is to bring about new things in the world. These things that are not just occupying space; they are fulfilling a purpose, and they have meaning on their own. To design is to create meaningful things for meaningful uses, understanding different uses and different materials.[15]

Design is a political, aesthetic, and moral activity.[16] Bringing new objects into the world has to be questioned as a political action—an intervention that modifies our presence in the world. Through objects, we engage with the world and with others, and the ways in which objects mediate that engagement make design an activity that can be understood as political or ethical.

Design is also an aesthetic activity, as functions are turned into forms and incarnated in the world as things.[17] Interaction with any object can have a purpose other than mere interaction: it can be beautiful, pleasurable, enriching. Design is not necessarily focused on creating beautiful things, but the importance of form is crucial for understanding the uniqueness of design as a way of engaging with the world.

The world itself must also be present in design. Again, design is as much understanding materiality as understanding the contexts of use in which that materiality is deployed and how they affect meaning and purpose. The relation between a designed thing and its context is a relation of resistance and occupation: the designed thing wants to focus and facilitate an action while eliminating the resistances that prevent that action from taking place.[18]

Design involves materiality and people, but also the economics, politics, and aesthetics of creation, production, consumption, and distribution. To design is to understand how to create things for people—things that are consumed, purchased, acquired, transmitted, enjoyed, suffered, and modified.

So from this perspective, what is game design? The design of games has been categorized as a type of emotional design[19] in which the creation of artificial obstacles enhances emotions through play.[20] However, I ask a different question: How can we create games that incorporate, allow, and encourage appropriative, creative, and disruptive play?

Let's go back to the notion of games and meaning. Much game design and game studies research has argued that games produce meaning because of a tight coupling between their rules and the messages they want to convey. Games are engaging, meaningful, activist, and important because their very form exists to prove it. Because games give strict form to play and someone has been in charge of designing that form, games can do things.

We still think about author, medium, communication, and channel. This is a valid interpretive framework if one accepts the idea of play as a protected activity created and guided by the rules of the game, oblivious of contexts, cultures, or player appropriation. This valid idea of play is tightly coupled to the also valid idea of games as formal systems.

However, in my ecology of play, the activity and the object are only loosely coupled. One cannot understand the playing of games without the rules of the game, but both are in constant motion toward and against each other; they are constantly redefined, negotiated, adapted, and denied by the other. The beauty, value, and politics of play reside precisely in the ways in which players solve this loose coupling, that is, the ways in which players engage with the ambiguous spaces between the rules and the actions and give meaning to their experience as it evolves over time. Playing is negotiating a wiggle space between rules, systems, contexts, preferences, appropriation, and submission.

So for this type of play, what kind of design can we apply? Designing for play means creating a setting rather than a system, a stage rather than a world, a model rather than a puzzle. Whatever is created has to be open, flexible, and malleable to allow players to appropriate, express, act and interact, make, and become part of the form itself.

Game design has sometimes been compared to architecture: the setting of a place with cues for behavior yet open for the users to modification. If we want this analogy to hold, if we want games that are architectural in spirit, then the idea of meaning needs to be abandoned in favor of collaborative processes of engagement and interaction among all agents in the network of play. Nobody dictates meaning, order, importance, or action; all agents, designers and players, negotiate play. The designer is just a stage setter, inviting others to play through this form that has been created or found. The designer's role is to open the gates for play in an object and with a purpose.

The designer of games should not act as a provider of anything other than context. A designer is a facilitator, a catalyst, but by no means does she possess the form she has created, for the form of play belongs only to those who engage with it—those who play. A game designer is not an author. Like a prop master or a stage director, the game designer proposes and deploys an object into the world, letting it speak for itself and be spoken through. These props not only do not resist appropriation; they encourage it and frame it as part of what it is to play.

The very notion of game designers is troublesome to me. It implies authorship, a privileged communication model, an implied authority or reference. At the same time, play is an affair of appropriation, of creation, of fluid margins and negotiations. A designer sets a frame for form to start its process, and then all other elements in the network take over, starting play as an act of creation and expression.

The word *designer*, then, seems to me inadequate for understanding the craft of creating forms for the activity of play. At the risk of being pedantic, I foolishly propose an alternative. Let us not talk about "game designers." Let us bury that terminology if what we are doing is not "games." If we are doing something else, if our purpose and our activity and our focus are to make people play, then let's become architects of play. Like architects, we create just contexts, and also like architects, we are slave to the ways others appropriate what we carefully create. We give a space for people to explore and express themselves and the right props to do so. We, the architects of play, make people play.

Game design is dead. Long live the architecture of play.

8 Play in the Era of Computing Machinery

What have computers ever done for us? They might have helped develop health care, security, commerce, transportation, and education to an extent that marks an era of prosperity and wealth previously unimaginable. But besides that, what have they ever done for us?

Well, they are the key elements of digital toys and digital games, which keep us, the modern developed world, entertained when we are not working. They have also become machines that can sense, interpret, and communicate with the environment, thus enriching the playful possibilities of toys and work devices. Computers have revolutionized play as much as they have all other domains in society. But what does this mean for our ecology of play? What is the relation between computation and play?

I start by describing what computers can do. Although we tend to give computers magical powers that turn them into cultural actors rather than "mere" technologies, a computer is a relatively simple machine that can do very few things very well. In essence, the computer excels at four things when we think about them for play:

1. A computer can perform calculations quickly and precisely. This capacity is useful in many different contexts, from rocket science to medical care. Its calculating power also allows it to create real-time simulations of complex systems, for instance, making worlds with coherent physics. Fast calculations also allow computers to act on complex input instantaneously. In Johan Sebastian Joust, the different machines involved (a conventional computer plus the embedded computers in the PlayStation Move controllers) calculate at high speed accelerometer data variations, effectively creating the challenges that make the game interesting. While the same play experience can be reproduced with analog resources, the use of computation gives Joust a different aesthetic experience, the magic feeling of having a lighted wand in your hands that reacts to movement and music.1 In Joust, computation enhances the aesthetics of play.

2. A computer can store large amounts of data while accessing them very quickly. This allows computers to act as externalized memory storages and also to create whole worlds with graphics, sounds, and computed behaviors. For those of us who love sports, the data immediacy that modern broadcasting offers has fundamentally changed the experience of watching any sport on television. While nothing beats the ritualistic communion with strangers that happens in an arena, sports broadcasting offers an enhanced, networked understanding of sports that contextualizes, explains, and even predicts actions while we are watching a game. Sports spectatorship has shifted from being essentially an affair in the present tense to a multilayered perspective in time and space, where actions take place now but are seen in the contexts of their past and their future.

3. A computer is equipped with a series of sensors programmed to sense its environment and turn analog input into computable

digital data. The computer on which I am writing this chapter has one high-definition camera, one microphone, and an accelerometer. It can see, feel, hear, and gather and process all those data. Similarly, most smart phones today know their geographical location, and some can even detect the proximity of other phones. Play, particularly toys, has greatly benefited from this computational sentience. A smart phone toy like Balloonimals makes use of accelerometer, touch, and microphone input to simulate playing with balloons. By providing touch and movement input, users can "inflate" and "shape" a virtual balloon, making it take the form of an animal.[2] Using the sensors on a smart phone, Balloonimals reproduces the creative activity of making shapes with balloons. Similarly, *Noby Noby Boy* playfully appropriates the sensors of the phone in order to make the act of mediating the world through those sensors a playful affair, making the camera take pictures that then become part of the digital toyful world of Boy.

4. A computer is often a part of a larger network of computers, which can help increase the previous three characteristics exponentially. Newstweek playfully appropriated the networked capacities of computers to tease our trust of online media. Part of this play happened with the network itself, with the connections between machines and the relations established among them. A computer is seldom alone: there's always traffic of data between machines that forms an alternative space we are only marginally aware of. The networks of computation are also our networks, our spaces for play.

Computers are, then, fast and efficient calculating machines that can process their analog environments into digital data they can perform operations with and are part of networks of data and information together with other computers.[3] They are also the embodiment of a way of understanding the world: because machines compute the world through systems, we might think that the world is actually a system composed of myriad subsystems.

We need therefore to think about the relations between systems and play and how play, in this the age of computing machinery, can coexist with computational thinking. The challenge for play in the era of computing machines is to learn to appropriate another dominant way of seeing the world—the systemic one.

Since computers are very good at calculation and data, provided the data are presented in a computable way, we have seen the emergence of a type of thinking that argues that the world can be understood through the description of the systems it is composed of. Thinking about the world as a collection of systems leads to a logical reduction of complexity, but also to new ways of understanding the world. For instance, cities are no longer irreducible collections of people and buildings and traffic and institutions and more; they are also patterns of systems that can be analyzed and described within different levels of abstraction. From there to *Sim City*, there is only one step: using a computer to simulate some of those systems. The affinity between this way of thinking and computation is striking: both benefit from the methodical reduction of complexity to systemic patterns that can be formalized.

This type of thinking has an extremely interesting impact on society, particularly in the way we address politics and even the ontology of human beings.[4] It is also a way of understanding and acting in a world closely connected to play as a mode of being. Both play and this type of understanding of systems, like reducing the world to patterns for behavior, also thrive in the emergence of rules.

The crucial difference between systems in this narrow sense and play is how play seeks appropriation, while system thinking thrives with reduction. This reduction is not necessarily a negative trait; it is a key of the scientific method. But it can be at odds with the performative aspects of play; play is action and performance, while "system thinking" is reduction and synthesis.

Computers are effective tools for practicing this type of systems-centric thinking, and they therefore reward designing for this type of experience of the world. But play requires other types of computational designs—more open, more attuned to the pleasures of performativity. By *performativity*, I am not exclusively reducing play to a bodily experience. As in the case of software toys and procedural toys, there is performative pleasure in tinkering with them to figure out what they do. In fact, there are arguably performative pleasures in the computational processes themselves. They are systems, but they are open to performing with them or performing themselves in a creative, expressive way, an openness in which they are playful.

The most interesting examples of performative playful processes are Twitter bots. Originally thought to be sleazy marketing tools (and still widely used for that purpose), bots in the hands of creators like Darius Kazemi have become proper computationally playful expressive devices that harness the inherent possibilities of computation as a form of expression and its role in our social and cultural contexts.[5]

A bot like Kazemi's *AmIRite*[6] playfully engages with Twitter's trending topics, rearranging them in creative and automated ways, quite often showing the needed absurdity of Twitter.[7] But even more, Twitter bots allow us to partially understand how computers see the world through their strict syntactical rules for the creation of sentences. What they say is, arguably, what they experience. We can playfully peek into the computational being's experiences through Twitter bots[8]—their playfulness being their only mode of existing in the world.

In the age of computing machinery, play and computational thinking need to help each other imagine new ways of being in the world. Computational systems need to be aware that they can be played with, that function and completeness are a consequence of the contexts in which they are deployed.[9] And play needs to benefit from the ways computing machinery can enhance our being in the world.

I have thought of play as a dance of resistance and appropriation, of creation and destruction of order. In the age of computing machinery, we need to see play as both playing systems and playing with systems, as appropriation and resistance of systems. Computers give us the pleasure of bound, limited, logical experiences; play gives the pleasure of breaking those boundaries and making them ours. Play allows us to reambiguate systems designed for clarity and efficiency. If system thinking creates patterns to explain, understand, and express the world, play appropriates to sometimes disrupt patterns for the sake of expression.

What, then, is the place of play in the era of computational machines? Computers are excellent play pals: their characteristics help us augment the world, delegate activities, and deputize users. Computers can provide an enhanced perception of the world, a different layer of data, and feedback that can contribute to play. In *Johan Sebastian Joust*, the software interprets motion and opens a space of possibility that is complementary to that created by the game.

Computers can help play take over the world. For its part, play needs to demand from computers more than the capacity to store and manipulate and move data: computers should take their place in the world and play *with us*—not for us, not against us, but together with us. Computation and play share some ontological traits, and so they should work together creating the beautiful spaces for play.

It is no surprise that the so-called ludic century is happening in the era of computing machinery. These calculating devices are more than aids. They open the world for interpretation, and the world is richer through computation. But to enjoy that richness, to take it and make it human, we need to express ourselves through it.[10] Computation can be human[11] only when we embrace it as what it is: not a technology but a modality of being, a form of expression.[12] Through play we embrace that possibility: play and computation are fellow travelers because both are ways of expressively being in the world.

There are risks: the capacity that computers have to relate the world to us can lead to the design of machines that addict us through play. Slot machines, video games, and even toys can give us both the pleasures of appropriative, creative play and an overtly focused being through systems. That encapsulated world of rewards and seemingly controllable chaos lies at the heart of the risks of play and computing. Even when it comes to their potential dangers, play and computation are closely connected; they simplify the world and make us crave that expressive simplification.

We don't need computing to play, and we don't need play for computation. But the alliance of computation and play, playing the world through computation or computing the world through play, are the most definite ways of defining the era of computing machinery.

Computers can do only a few things well: compute fast vast amounts of data while sensing the world and being in a network. Through these capacities, computers can make sense of the world and augment it, expanding the physical context into an informational context. All of these characteristics can be appropriated through play for expressive reasons: data and sensors facilitate the sensual play of *Johan Sebastian Joust*; networks and data are manipulated in Newstweek; *Noby Noby Boy* lives of the world captured and translated by a tiny portable computer. There is more than the world to playfully take over now: there's the world, the machines, and the way the machines make the world exist. There is more to take over, and more interesting, machines are not active accomplices in this appropriation.

In fact, what computer programs do is appropriate a machine and express themselves to it—hence the natural relations between play and computation. A computer is a universal Turing machine that can be programmed to become any other Turing machine. It is a machine that is programmed to take over and express itself through another machine. Programming a computer is making it play—that is, be another machine. So let's be bold: all computation is play.

Play is appropriation, expression, and a personal affair. Together with computation, they bring us an expanded world with which we can play, that we can make ours as we delegate to and appropriate machines. Play has always done that, but only play in the era of computing machinery has the opportunity to connect us to a whole world besides the world in which we play. So in this era of computing machines for play, what have computers actually done for us? They have opened a new world to play with while being at play.

....

We have now reached the end of this trip. I have sketched the map of an ecology of play, a world of playthings and spaces and computers where we play to express who we are and what we can do. This expression will make the world ours through play, making our memories flow and giving us places to remember, people to love, and knowledge and wisdom and foolishness. We are what and how and where and with whom we play, our mark in the world and in time.

Play gives us the world, and through play we make the world ours.

Notes

Chapter 1

1. The most convincing academic argument on the topic is Juul's *A Casual Revolution* (2009), which focuses on the success of casual games and how they have expanded the audience for computer games.

2. The champion of this idea is Eric Zimmerman, who specified it in a manifesto in late 2013: http://kotaku.com/manifesto-the-21st-century -will-be-defined-by-games-1275355204 (accessed October 16, 2013). This idea, however, had already been popular, with different phrasings, in game developer venues such as the annual Game Developers Conference. Game designer Clint Hocking provided a useful summary and insightful critique of the ludic century ideal in his blog in late 2011: http://www.clicknothing.com/click_nothing/2011/11/redacted-the-dominant-cultural-form-of-the-21st-century.html (accessed November 22, 2011).

3. Heather Chaplin and Eric Zimmerman presented this idea at the 2008 Games + Learning + Society conference, later to be published as Zimmerman's manifesto (see note 2).

4. This book is written as an update to the tradition of Huizingan play, a canon consisting roughly of Huizinga (1992), Sutton-Smith (1997), DeKoven (2002), Caillois (2001), and Suits (2005). The update will consist of an expansion of the theories used to explain play, as well as a focus on materiality and design: how the objects of play, the playthings, are designed to help us engage with the world through play.

5. Isaacson (2011).

6. Huizinga remains a central figure in the understanding of play, and although the theory of play I am presenting here is markedly post-Huizingan, it is still very much affected by his ideas. Homo Ludens was Huizinga's interpretation of a third dominant anthropology of humans. If *Homo sapiens* was the being or reason, and *Homo faber* the being of production, *Homo ludens* would be the being of play. This being would also be responsible for the play element in culture, which in Huizinga's view was at the center of Western culture. Play, mostly understood as ritual, had an imprint in the configuration of history and culture that needed to be defined, and so play needed understanding too. Huizinga's ideas, only moderately influential outside cultural anthropology, are still informing our understanding of play, despite the fact that *Homo Ludens* is a relatively outdated book (for a critical review of the text, see Henricks 2006).

7. To be fair, this idea is also present in Huizinga. However, his insistence on play being separate from real life weakens the creative and expressive capacities of play, as it can be understood only within the bound context of its own performance, and not within the larger context in which people play, or the multiplicity of intentions behind this activity.

8. Caillois (2001) writes about the idea of the corruption of play and its potential dangers in chapter 4 of *Man, Play and Games*. Sutton-Smith (1997) dedicates some critical thoughts to gambling and cruel play.

9. These ideas are explored in Nietzsche's *The Birth of Tragedy* (1872, 1993).

10. As presented in Schechner (1988). For an annotated introduction to the use of the concept of play in performance studies, see Schechner (2006).

11. While Schechner provides interesting examples of dark play, I contribute with one example I expand on later in this book. When playing the game *B.U.T.T.O.N.*, some players might be compelled to exert more physical violence than others. For some, that violence is part of the

play, and in playing, that is manifested as an act of dark play: it is unclear if the tackling responds to an interpretation of how to play the game or a different desire. It is an exploration of the boundaries created by this game. See also Wilson (2011).

12. Understood in the sense of Russian literary theorist Bakhtin (1984, 2008).

13. "The feast was a temporary suspension of the entire official system with all its prohibitions and hierarchic barriers. For a short time life came out of its usual, legalized and consecrated furrows and entered the sphere of utopian freedom" (Bakhtin 1984, 89).

14. "Next to the universality of medieval laughter we must stress another striking peculiarity: its indissoluble and essential relation to freedom.... This freedom of laughter was, of course, relative; its sphere was at times wider and at times narrower, but it was never entirely suspended" (Bakhtin 1984, 89). Where Bakhtin writes about laughter, I write about carnivalesque play, which I claim is similar; in fact, laughter is a manifestation of carnivalesque play.

15. Twitter bots are essentially computer programs designed to generate tweets and post them on that social network. And if you don't know what I am talking about, read this piece by Sarah Brin: http://nybots .tumblr.com/post/62834461397/who-led-the-horse-to-ebooks (accessed October 17, 2013).

16. By *postromantic*, I am referring to the focus that particularly game aesthetics pays to the notions of authorship, form, and individual expression.

17. In this sense, this work is close to that of critical designers like Dunne (2006), Sengers and Gaver (2006), Sengers et al. (2005), and Hallnäs and Redström (2001).

18. Not strictly from an etiological perspective such as those presented by Schechner (1988); however, I am interested in play not as a biological manifestation but as a cultural manifestation.

19. "Maybe scholars should declare a moratorium on defining play" (Schechner 1988, 3).

20. Besides this temporal framework, my minimalist understanding of play also wants to stay away from the essentialist approach that many humanistic thinkers take when trying to understand sociocultural phenomena. I am trying to understand play and why it matters, but I am not trying to formally define play. If anything, my definition is indebted to the work in sociology that has seen play within its cultural, social context. This book owes much to Henricks's *Play Reconsidered* (2006), though my approach is both more humanistic and more interested in the objects of play, and they lead eventually to questions on design and materiality. However, it is my intention to provide a nonessentialist take on defining play.

21. The notion of context is a dangerous one. A word commonly used in sociological studies, *context* is often applied to the understanding of everything that surrounds the human action that is relevant for a situation (Goffman 1959; for an overview of the topic, Ritzer 2000 is a very good textbook). My understanding of context, though, is willingly different. I am inspired by the work of Bruno Latour (1992), and other actor-network theorists (Latour 2005; Law and Hassard 1999), but I am also closer to the postphenomenological tradition of Verbeek (2006), which tries to see technologies in context as part of our way of experiencing and constructing the world. In this theory of play, context encompasses the social, cultural, technological, and physical situatedness of play and how objects are an integral part of what play is. In this sense, then, I am closer to an understanding of context that also introduced some elements of classic ubiquitous computing literature, particularly the work of Dourish (2001, 2004). More specifically, I think that my understanding of context is close to Dourish's understanding of "practice": "By turning our attention from 'context' (as a set of descriptive features of settings) to 'practice' (forms of engagement with those settings), we assigned a central role to the meanings that people find in the world and the meanings of their actions there in terms of the consequences and interpretations of those actions for themselves and for others" (2004, 27–28). I stick, however, to the concept of context because of its colloquial clarity.

22. In texts on soccer (J. Wilson 2008; Goldblatt 2006), there is often a discussion of the source of great football: Does it come from the street-

wise kids who learn to dribble while playing in open public spaces with no age or skill segregation, or is it something nurtured in scientific training in academies? The Argentinian fascination for *potrero* soccer (played by slum kids who make it to the top and, possibly, a consequence of Diego Armando Maradona's sociocultural impact, since *El Diego* is arguably the best player of all time, and is himself of extremely humble origins) is somewhat opposite to the classic Dutch focus on training at an early age. These approaches yield different play styles, that is, different individual and collective interpretations of playing the game of soccer.

23. Again, this idea is close to Dourish's understanding of context: "As competent social actors in particular domains, we can find the world and the settings we encounter as meaningful. This unification of action and meaning is also central to the question of context, since context is essentially about the ways in which actions can be rendered as meaningful—how a particular action, for example, becomes meaningful for others by dint of where it was performed, when, or with whom" (2004, 24).

24. This is, of course, an interpretation of the classic design research concepts of affordances and constraints (Norman 2002), though I'd claim that objects designed for play, or *playthings*, answer better to the notion of designed signifiers that Norman introduced in *Living with Complexity* (2010).

25. In the next chapter I write about how playfulness is an attitude that allows different interpretations of nonplay contexts. A very simple example is the Apple computer. Apple's focus on making computing machines feel playful, filling them with animations and quirks, suggests a different attitude from the user than toward a conventional gray-box computer. This was one of the core design drives of Steve Jobs, and a good example of how a playful attitude can be invoked in contexts that do not necessarily involve, or lead to, play.

26. Since I understand play as a form of expression akin to language (as does Sutton-Smith, 1997, 219: "Play is like a language: a system of communication and expression, not in itself either good or bad"), I take that as a term of comparison. Languages are not designed, or at least not in the same ways play is designed for. By *designed*, here, I am referring to

the capacity of humans for artificially creating playthings that aid the activity of play. It is an understanding of design as a science of the artificial (Simon 1996, but specially Cross 2007), as the collection of knowledge, skills, and insights that leads to the creation of objects that contribute to the experience of being in the world (Verbeek, 2006).

27. Pye (1978) has an idea of the aesthetics of design that is deeply influenced by the importance of form and function in the creation of the objects. It is still a surprisingly popular approach, even though usability gurus like Norman (2004) have distanced themselves from this modernist idea.

28. This is one of the foci of the initial chapter of *Homo Ludens*, as well as the usual topic in many game studies books (Salen and Zimmerman 2004; Juul 2005). See also Henricks (2006, 209–212) and the formalist works of Avedon (1971). Also, the study of rules cannot avoid the importance of Wittgenstein (1961, 1991).

29. Readers will recognize here the work of Goffman (1961).

30. This attitude toward play has been mentioned by Huizinga, Caillois, and Sutton-Smith, but it is Suits (2005) who named it "the lusory attitude." DeKoven (2002) bases much of his work on understanding this attitude and how it is malleable, changing with the context and purpose of the playful activity.

31. Unlike what Huizinga (1992) thought: "The rules of a game are absolutely binding and allow no doubt.... As soon as the rules are transgressed the whole play-world collapses" (11). Unlike Huizinga, I'd claim that in many cases when the rules are transgressed, new play worlds emerge.

32. Examples abound: house rules, self-imposed challenges (http://drgamelove.blogspot.com/2009/12/permanent-death-complete-saga.html), and even sports tactics: they are all interpretations of rules in order to facilitate play.

33. Again, Huizinga (1992): "The player who trespasses against the rules or ignores them is a 'spoil-sport.' ... He must be cast out, for he threatens the existence of the play-community" (11).

34. All the works of the New Games movement, the late 1960s movement that wanted to encourage more playful, noncompetitive games, are within this interpretive frame, particularly those of DeKoven, for whom playing is more important than playing by the rules.

35. This idea is adapted from the original concept of orderly and disorderly play that Henricks (2009) proposed.

36. As Nietzsche argued for in *The Birth of Tragedy* (1993). I am aware that this is a work of the young Nietzsche, and very much a text written as a particular response to a cultural and artistic climate. However, the dichotomy between the Apollonian and the Dionysiac is, as I will argue, relevant for understanding play, even though it implies a certain freedom of interpretation of the original concepts.

37. Nietzsche (1993) writes: "And let us now imagine how the ecstatic sound of the Dionysiac revels echoed ever more enticingly around this world, built on illusion and *moderation*, and artificially restrained— how their clamor voiced all the *excess* of nature in delight, suffering, and knowledge, and even in the most piercing cry: imagine what the psalmodizing apolline artist, with his phantom harpnotes, could have meant compared to this daemonic folk song" (26). Incidentally, the rise of physical indie games that are inspired by folk games like *B.U.T.T.O.N* (folk games are understood to be popular games that are played in groups and transmitted through communities of play), and the presence of folk games in many indie events (such as IndieCade, the yearly festival of independent games), could be interpreted as a Dionysiac reaction to the Apollonian presence of computer games (formal systems running on computing machines) that dominated the late twentieth century.

38. "Play is characteristically buoyant and disrespectful, and players are indulgent in the broadest sense of that term. Committed to living in the present, players insert their interests and enthusiasms wherever possible. Within the boundaries of the event itself, action typically dances and darts. We demolish our carefully constructed castle of blocks and are fascinated by the clatter of its collapse" (Henricks 2006, 205–206).

39. Huizinga (1992) mentions the importance of play as a creator of order, an Apollonian footprint that can still be felt today in the way we

think about play. See, for example, Koster's *A Theory of Fun for Game Design* (2005) and its hypothesis that playing is akin to learning since it consists of pattern recognition behaviors. We learn, and play, by recognizing order—a valid way of understanding play, but only one possible way of acknowledging the ways in which play matters.

40. There is a certain pleasure in rational, goal-oriented play. While instrumental play can be a highly positive type of play (Taylor 2006a), it can also lead to worse instances of instrumental play (Sicart 2012), in which the very purpose of play is lost in external rewards and mindless interactions.

41. "Play can be deferred or suspended at any time" (Huizinga, 1992, 8).

42. Bakhtin (1984, 2008). Incidentally, the presence of Bakhtin can also be felt in some design research work. See, for example, Wright, Wallace, and McCarthy (2008).

43. This is not a totally new idea in play studies: "Festive events are typically an alternation between patterns of aggressive, creative activity and its opposite—a more receptive and adaptive mode" (Henricks 2006, 92). However, the application of Bakhtin's carnival and its important ties to ideas of modernity and freedom separates my work from other theories of play.

44. See also Schmitz (1988): "Like art and religion, play is not far from the feast, for art celebrates beauty and religion celebrates glory, but play celebrates the emergence of a finite world that lies outside and beyond the world of nature while at the same time resting upon it" (33). Similarly, see Fink (1988) or Esposito (1988).

45. "Laughter at the feast of fools was not, of course, an abstract and purely negative mockery of the Christian ritual and the Church's hierarchy. The negative derisive element was deeply immersed in the triumphant theme of bodily regeneration and renewal. It was 'man's second nature' that was laughing, the lower bodily stratum which could not express itself in official cult and ideology" (Bakhtin 1984, 75). And, "the feast was a temporary suspension of the entire official system with all its prohibitions and hierarchic barriers. For a short time life came out of its

usual, legalized and consecrated furrows and entered the sphere of utopian freedom" (89).

46. "The Renaissance conception of laughter can be roughly described as follows: Laughter has a deep philosophical meaning, it is one of the essential forms of the truth concerning the world as a whole, concerning history and man; it is a peculiar point of view relative to the world; the world is seen anew, no less (and perhaps more) profoundly than when seen from the serious standpoint. Therefore, laughter is just as admissible in great literature, posing universal problems, as seriousness. Certain essential aspects of the world are accessible only to laughter" (Bakhtin 1984, 66).

47. "In other words, medieval laughter became at the Renaissance stage of its development the expression of a new free and critical *historical* consciousness" (Bakhtin 1984, 73).

48. "Seriousness was therefore elementally distrusted, while trust was placed in festive laughter" (Bakhtin 1984, 95).

49. "Laughter is essentially not an external but an interior form of truth; it cannot be transformed into seriousness without destroying and distorting the very contents of the truth which it unveils. Laughter liberates not only from external censorship but first of all from the great interior censor; it liberates from the fear that developed in man during thousands of years: fear of the sacred, of prohibitions, of the past, of power. It unveils the material bodily principle in its true meaning" (Bakhtin 1984, 94).

50. "The images of games were seen as a condensed formula of life and of the historic process: fortune, misfortune, gain and loss, crowning and uncrowning.... At the same time games drew the players out of the bounds of everyday life, liberated them from usual laws and regulations, and replaced established conventions by other lighter conventionalities.... The peculiar interpretation of games in Rabelais' time must be carefully considered. Games were not as yet thought of as a part of ordinary life and even less of its frivolous aspect. Instead they had preserved their philosophical meaning" (Bakhtin 1984, 235–236).

51. "Play is usually thought to be a time when people 'take over' their own affairs.... In play, so it is argued, people can have the world to their liking.... Play gives people a chance to shape the world—and to do so according to their own terms and timing" (Henricks 2006, 7–8).

52. Also known as Ninja Slap: http://www.urbandictionary.com/define. php?term=Ninja%20Slap (accessed December 1, 2011). See also http:// ultimateninjacombat.com/ (accessed December 1, 2011).

53. http://gutefabrik.com/joust.html (accessed December 1, 2011).

54. Incidentally, appropriative play also happens in the case of spectatorship. Sports are a case in which the appropriative nature of play can be used to understand the ways in which we contemplate play. To see a game being played, a sport or something like Ninja or *Joust,* is also to participate, to play—a minor, perhaps secondary way, but also a way of performing the basic appropriative move that defines play as an activity.

55. A Marxist would probably be proud of this interpretation of play, following Henricks's (2006) exegesis of Marx: "Indeed, the objects themselves are much less important than the experience of human relationship that derives from the activity" (37).

56. http://camover.noblogs.org. See also http://www.disinfo.com/2013 /01/camover-a-game-to-destroy-cctv-cameras/ and http://www.guardian .co.uk/theguardian/shortcuts/2013/jan/25/game-destroy-cctv-cameras-berlin (accessed February 1, 2013).

57. In Schechner's own words, "Dark play subverts order, dissolves frames, breaks its own rules, so that the playing itself is in danger of being destroyed, as in spying, con-games, undercover actions, and double agentry. Unlike the inversions of carnivals, ritual clowns, and so on (whose agendas are public), dark play's inversions are not declared or resolved; its end is not integration but disruption, deceit, excess, and gratification" (1988, 13).

58. "Play creates its own (permeable) boundaries and realms: multiple realities that are slippery, porous, and full of creative lying and deceit; that play is dangerous and, because it is, players need to feel secure in

order to begin playing; that the perils of playing are often masked or disguised by saying that play is fun, voluntary, a leisure activity, or ephemeral—when in fact the fun of playing, when there is fun, is in playing with fire, going in over one's head, inverting accepted procedures and hierarchies; that play is performative involving players, directors, spectators, and commentators" (Schechner, 1988, 5).

59. And not only adult play, but also children's play, as Sutton-Smith has already noted (1997, 111–123).

60. Schüll's (2012) work on the design of gambling machines is particularly fascinating: "From virtual reel mapping and disproportionate reels to video slots' asymmetric reels; from the illusory player control conveyed by stop buttons and joysticks to the illusory offs conveyed by teaser strips: These methods, supported by a whole corporate, legal, and regulatory apparatus, gave machine designers greater control over the odds and presentation of chance while fostering enchanting 'illusions of control', distorted perception of odds, and near-miss effects among gamblers. In what amounts to a kind of enchantment by design, finely tuned, chance-mediating technologies function as 'really new gods', captivating their audience" (95).

61. See also Henricks's (2006, particularly pages 169–170) reading of the works of Goffman.

62. "What does seem distinctive about play is the degree to which the characteristic rationale for the activity ... is contained or restricted within the activity itself. To play is to acknowledge that this restricted sphere is a legitimate place to operate, that people can passionately pursue objectives here without interference or condemnation from other spheres. There will be personal or social consequences for what occurs.... However, these consequences are for the most part kept 'in the room'" (Henricks 2006, 191).

63. See Suits (1988): "*All* instances of play *are* instances of autotelic activity" (19).

64. This is of course a jab against the idea of magic circle, which is a common (mis)interpretation of Huizinga's proposal of autotelic play.

See Consalvo (2009). Goffman's ideas can also be used to destabilize the idea of magic circle: "Games in fact have boundaries that are semi-permeable. Certain issues inevitably come through" (Henricks 2006, 151).

65. http://mightyvision.blogspot.dk/2012/08/vesper5.html.

66. Again, the influence of actor-network theory should be clear here. I understand the activity of play as taking place in an ecology of things, people, and processes, all of which are related in multiple and varying ways through time. The purpose of a theory of play should be to identify the workings of these networks and propose a vocabulary that allows for approaching instances of the activity in meaningful, critical ways.

67. "To play a game is to reclaim suddenly experiences he has had before or even, more profoundly, to retrace the steps of anyone who has ever played the game" (Henricks 2006, 13).

68. "To play is to know that there is a wider world—with all its obligations and complexities- just beyond the gates of the playground. Furthermore, this wider world is needed to give play its sense of urgency and meaning. From those external settings, people import the frequently contradictory values and challenges of their times as well as their own more general issues about personal functioning" (Henricks 2006, 219). Also, in the way I understand the ecology of play, postphenomenological thinking has a lot of weight: through playthings, we experience play, and they have a role in shaping the activity in the ways they mediate it, but also in the ways they open themselves to being interpreted, questioned, appropriated.

69. "The realm of play, if participated in openly, offers obvious opportunities to explore alternative modes of awareness, to develop insights into and knowledge of new modes of being, and to explore radically different possibilities perhaps not readily available elsewhere" (Meier 1988, 194).

70. The careful reader will have probably noticed how I've eluded the classic notion of play as being "voluntary." The more I think about play, the less I see the notion of voluntary as being an important ontological

mark of it. It is true that we often choose to play, but the initial choice may be followed by playing without the intention of playing, just for social pressure. Play is an activity we often engage with voluntarily, but voluntariness does not define the activity: play can happen, and it often does, without being a choice on the part of the players. It is, once again, a remnant of Huizinga's idealized vision of play that often leads us to think about play as *obligatory* voluntary.

71. "As soon as a man apprehends himself as free and wishes to use his freedom, a freedom, by the way, which could just as well be his anguish, then his activity is play" (Sartre 1988, 169).

72. "To play is to take an explanatory attitude toward being at all times" (Fink 1988, 105).

73. Sartre (1988, 170).

Chapter 2

1. The idea of software appropriating the hardware, and the potential political, legal, and ethical implications, are explained by Lessig (2000), though more pertinent analysis of the relations between software and hardware can be found in Bogost and Montfort (2009) or Wardrip-Fruin (2009). However, the most interesting insights on the relation between software and hardware are often found in science and technology studies (see Latour 1992, 2005). See also Kittler (2010).

2. Although this is not the place to discuss these matters, an interesting thread that needs to be explored when thinking about the relations between play and the digital domain is that of the role of gatekeepers in the shaping of playful technologies. For all the potentialities that an iPhone presents, it is ultimately the corporation that produced it, Apple, that allows software to run on it. The way this institutional presence affects the inherent freedom of play should be a subject of interest for researchers and creators of digital play.

3. Sports cars are often marketed as this kind of emotional playful devices, like the Mazda Zoom Zoom campaign (http://zoom-zoom

.mazda.com/, accessed December 9, 2011); thanks to Mark J. Nelson for this observation. Similarly, the use of colors in household appliances (see, e.g., the Danish brand Bodum: http://www.bodum.com/dk/da/shop/prodlist/30/, accessed December 9, 2011) elevates them from dull instruments for food production to part of the sensory experience of cooking. Marketing theorists have written extensively and appropriately about "playful consumption" and how it can be leveraged in the marketplace (see Holbrook and Hirschman 1982; Holbrook et al. 1984; Grayson 1999; Molesworth and Denegri-Knot 2008).

4. See Blijlevens, Creusen, and Schoormans (2009) for an account on marketing, design, and emotions.

5. The rise of gamification as a concept in 2010 is testimony to this idea—that through play and its values, businesses and services can better engage consumers. Gamification in its commercial phrasing was widely criticized, yet there is still some hope in thinking about playfulness outside the domain of formalized play. See Deterding et al. (2011a, 2011b) for a complete, thorough, and hopeful critique of the gamification.

6. Sports car commercials often present the product in a playful way. Similarly, worldwide brands such as Apple ("Think Different"), HP ("The Computer Is Personal, Again"), and Nike ("Just do it," and particularly its football commercials of the late 1990s with Eric Cantona as a star: http://www.youtube.com/watch?v=egNMC6YfpeE ; http://www.youtube.com/watch?v=vdhvp-iYR3s; accessed December 9, 2011) use the rhetoric of play to engage their potential customers by appealing to a different set of values from those often applied to their commercial domains (computing, sports).

7. A typical example is the publicity for caffeinated energy drinks, which dress themselves as sporting radical lifestyles even though the drinks are an important part of modern performance enhancers in the workplace.

8. This is resonant of the Frankfurt school approach to modernity. See Adorno and Horkheimer (2010).

9. This definition of playfulness is inspired by Lieberman's work (1977), though my approach is less sociological, and probably less influenced by Goffman and other sociological theorists and more imbued with the rhetorics of playful design and performance studies.

10. This reference is close to Debord's situationist international and their interest in political playfulness. Wark's (2011) excellent summary of the movement is a good introduction to the topic, though some readers may be familiar with Debord's idea of détournement (Debord and Wolman 2009).

11. The attraction and pleasures of labor are already well observed by Marx in both its economic and cultural importance. Henricks's (2006) detailed reading of Marx through the lens of play contributes to understanding the instrumental pleasures of formalized work and how those pleasures are akin to the result of play. Of course, Adorno's (2004) resistance to these pleasures and his idea of how aesthetics can free us can be relevant for understanding these pleasures.

12. See Henricks (2006): "Playful expression tends to be organized as a series of pleasant individual escapades or interludes, officially permitted departures from public routine. In this way, even the 'escape routes' for public expression have been anticipated and prepared by formal organizations" (106).

13. Besides the work on marketing and playfulness and Lieberman's book (1977), the notion of playfulness is also present in design research (Gaver 2009; Nam and Kim 2011), critical theory (Benjamin 1999d; Adorno 2004) and performance studies (Schechner 2006). The idea of play as an activity is independent of the ideas proposed by activity theory, though some inspiration was drawn from Kaptelinin and Nardi (2006), particularly in the importance of the sociocultural and technical contexts in the practice of both play and playfulness.

14. The idea of frames refers to Goffman (1959), even though, as Henricks (2006) points out, "[Goffman's playfulness] refers primarily to various forms of imaginative role play that sometimes interrupt the flow of social interaction" (164), rather than to a different activity or attitude than that of play.

15. By "resisting" here I am referring to the fact that even though some attitudes are often guided toward objects or contexts, these worldly domains may ignore our attitudes. Verbeek (2006) gives the example of speed bumps and speed radars, and how they incite violent responses from drivers. The machines, the things, resist the attitude of the drivers, who cannot impose their will on those machines. Playful designs are a negotiation, a dance of this resistance, oscillating between acceptance of playfulness and rejection of actions that don't lead to the desired outcomes (see Sengers et al. 2005 for a reflection on this type of design approach from a human–computer interaction perspective and Gaver et al. 2009 for a critical reflection on the success of these approaches).

16. This idea is present in some of the philosophy of sports dedicated to the aesthetic ideal; see Morgan and Meier (1988).

17. See http://online.wsj.com/news/articles/SB10001424127887323375 20457826991660836834 (accessed October 17, 2013).

18. I designed a game around this very premise: http://deterbold.com/ catastrophes/dead-drops/.

19. A video of the famous penalty can be seen here: http://www .youtube.com/watch?v=Bd1Hr96IenI (accessed December 9, 2011).

20. See, for instance, Brown and Duguid (1994), Newton (2004), Taylor (2006a), and Turkle (2007). Despite their different methodological traditions, all of these texts share a certain critical perspective on the relations between technology and humans. Outside of design research or science and technology studies, the work of postphenomenologists provides equally interesting insights on the relation between technologies and practices.

21. http://www.tinkerkit.com/fake-computer-real-violence   (accessed February 4, 2013).

22. http://accidentalnewsexplorer.com/ (accessed December 10, 2011).

23. There is dark playfulness like there is dark play, and it is not my intention to be normative about it. In fact, dark playfulness is likely to be an interesting approach to understanding politics through technolo-

gies and actions, as in the playful use of billboards by the Billboard Liberation Front (http://www.billboardliberation.com/, accessed December 10, 2011) or many of Banksy's works, which are much more context dependent than what photographical records may show (his work in the Gaza strip is an example: http://arts.guardian.co.uk/pictures /0,,1543331,00.html; accessed December 10, 2011).

24. http://www.stfj.net/art/2009/best%20day%20ever/   (accessed December 10, 2011).

25. There are resonances between this idea and Goffman's theories: "Goffman posits a continuum between play and games. Play is typically a temporary transformation of some practical activity. An ordinary object suddenly becomes a 'play-thing' and is abandoned just as quickly" (Henricks 2006, 165). I am not arguing here for a continuity between play and games, but for understanding games as props for play (or, in a weakest sense, games as the form of play). Hence, Goffman's insights are only marginally useful.

26. http://www.doodlebuzz.com/ (accessed December 10, 2011).

27. I am indebted to Sebastian Möring for this concept.

28. Incidentally, they can also be contexts modified for play, such as spaces taken over by play. For instance, the space around foosball tables at IT University is often transformed during leisure hours into improvised stadiums for hard competition. The context of the public space of a university is modified to accommodate a play activity.

29. Compare, for example, the initial release of Apple's Keynote presentation software with the version of Microsoft's PowerPoint available at that time: Apple's focus on animations, images, and videos, as well as the care for design and typography, made Keynote a much more playful presentation software.

30. http://www.liveplasma.com/.

31. http://www.twittearth.com/.

32. http://julianoliver.com/output/packet-garden.

33. http://newstweek.com/.

34. http://www.wikihow.com/Make-Moss-Graffiti.

35. I am here referring to classic works such as Dreyfuss (2003) and Pye (1978). Norman's *The Design of Everyday Things* (2002) is a usability take on functionalist thinking and therefore also part of the tradition I am referring to.

36. I am not blind to the commercial angle of this reflection: lack of personality eases the turnaround of new household projects.

37. "People appropriate and reinterpret systems to produce their own uses and meanings, and these are frequently incompatible with design expectations and inconsistent within and across groups" (Sengers and Gaver 2006, 3).

38. That is, the system is not guaranteeing functionality: "Systems that are open to interpretation don't need to be tailored to fit every possible niche audience; instead, the same system may support many ways of experiencing and acting in the world" (Sengers and Gaver 2006, 3).

39. "In our culture, technology often carries connotations of precision, correctness, and authority which can make users feel that the system's apparent interpretation (e.g., the data it collects and presents) must be more correct than users' own understandings" (Sengers and Gaver 2006, 6).

40. This is the idea behind Dunne's (2006) user-unfriendliness concept.

41. These are better explained by Gaver et al. (2004), who write that playful technologies are meant to "promote curiosity," "de-emphasize the pursuit of external goals," "maintain openness and ambiguity," "support social engagement in social activities," and "allow the ludic to be interleaved with everyday utilitarian activities."

42. While I am aware that this may sound like a harsh criticism, there is an important issue at stake: the idea of playful design is important, and its proponents argue for its current success in the world of design. However, there is a certain disconnect between the ideas, the implementations, and the actual presence of these radically playful technologies in

our everyday technological use. For playful design to be as successful as Gaver (2009) claims, it should be present in many more technologies than it is now. It's true that we're witnessing a shift toward playfulness in technology, but the presence and role of institutional gatekeepers prevent the focus on ambiguity to prevail.

43. Dunne's works, as revolutionary and interesting as they are, still take place and space in the art gallery. Interestingly, the method of cultural probes, developed between Gaver and Dunne, is actually quite popular in playful design companies such as IDEO.

44. Many of the interesting answers are collected in the blog "Shit Siri Says" (http://shitsirisays.com/, accessed December 12, 2011). More interesting, and politically relevant, is how a glitch in Siri prevented it from giving directions to abortion clinics (http://www.cbsnews. com/8301-501465_162-57334773-501465/siris-abortion-answers-are-a-glitch-says-apple/, accessed December 12, 2011). Winner (1986), Latour (1992), and Verbeek (2006) provide interesting angles to explain this embedded politics in design.

45. Again, there is an obvious commercial side to it: when disposing of an Apple product equipped with Siri, we cannot but think that we're actually *disposing of Siri*. The personal attachment to this playful companion can be an extraordinary market tool that might prevent users from leaving the platform on emotional grounds.

Chapter 3

1. Except Sutton-Smith, who dedicated a volume to toys (Sutton-Smith 1986), all other major play theorists, from Huizinga to DeKoven, focused on games as the form of play, paying little to no attention to toys. Ironically, critical theory (Benjamin 1999a, b, c) and literary theory (Stewart 1993) have given due importance to the cultural role of toys in the context of play.

2. In the three texts from which this chapter draws inspiration (Sutton-Smith 1986; Benjamin 1999a; Stewart 1993), toys are defined only in oblique ways. It seems that, much like play, there is something obvious

with the colloquial use of the concept of toy that makes it difficult and paradoxically trivial to define *toy*. Intuitively we know what toys are. In this chapter, I keep that ambiguity alive, so I will not propose a formal definition of *toy*, but I will describe toys from both a cultural and a technological perspective.

3. The authors of the texts that inspire this chapter seldom question the materiality of the toy. There are interesting insights in Benjamin's work, but most of the time he does not question the toy as a thing. However, in order to insert toys into this ecology of play, their very materiality, the way they act as playthings, is fundamental. The portable theory of play I am proposing here requires paying attention to the "thingness" of things as much as to their cultural roles. In this sense, the chapter diverges from Benjamin, Sutton-Smith, and Stewart in the attention to the material conditions that make toys a plaything.

4. http://o--o.jp/.

5. http://www.danieldisselkoen.nl/man-eater/ (accessed February 5, 2013).

6. Anybody who has looked in awe at a model train or at *Sim City* knows how these types of mechanical toys, in their alterity, are fascinating devices to look at; they are tiny worlds that paradoxically seem to operate on appropriately scaled-down versions of the same laws our physical world obeys. In Stewart's (1993) words, "The toy world presents a projection of the world of everyday life; this real world is miniaturized or gigantized in such a way as to test the relation between materiality and meaning. We are thrilled and frightened by the mechanical toy because it presents the possibility of a self-invoking fiction, a fiction which exists independent of human signifying processes" (1993, 57).

7. I appropriate the concept of procedurality as coined by Murray (1998) and Bogost (2007), since it explains how some toys are created to reproduce in different scale processes, from trains to cities to steam engines. Instead of the complicated terms of simulation, simulacra, and other loaded concepts, procedurality allows me to focus on how these toys are created with a set of processes in mind—processes that define them—and that on occasion can be performed without any human

presence. Model toys, and software toys like *The Sims* and *Sim City* fall into this category of procedural toys.

8. In classic design research terms, the fascination produced by procedural toys can be explained by how they obscure the system image, forcing us to reconstruct it as a playful process; in other words, making the user image becomes a play process (see Norman 2002).

9. "Toys can be thought of scientifically as a series of object ideoglyphs of modern object reality" (Sutton-Smith 1986, 243), and, "What we need to realize is that whatever the type of play, it is partly because the toy is a schematic and familiar signal that the players can treat it in their own preferred way" (Sutton-Smith 1986, 250).

10. http://www.flong.com/projects/yellowtail/ (accessed February 5, 2013).

11. A sketch of this history can be found in Benjamin (1999b).

12. See Sutton-Smith (1986): "The development of the modern concept of toy seems to have occurred first between the years 1550 and 1750 when the new idea of the industrial machine began to change the nature of the world" (58), and, "The modern toy may be seen in part as a symbolic legatee of this first optimistic scientific view of the planned universe. In its smallness the toy, along with other miniatures, represented a departure from the thousands of years in which the major 'science' for the peoples of the world was the science of largeness, of the macrocosm, of astronomy" (59).

13. See Benjamin (1999b): "Here, perhaps, is the deepest explanation for the two meanings of the German word *Spielen*: the element of repetition is what is actually common to them. Not a 'doing as if' but a 'doing the same thing over and over again,' the transformation of a shattering experience into habit—that is the essence of play" (120). This idea resonates powerfully in Adorno's (2004) aesthetic theory.

14. Formalized in the Huizingian sense that games are the form of play, an analysis that Caillois (2001) reiterates and that is also present in Schechner's (1988) understanding of play in relation to rituals. The main issue with this focus on formalized play is, again, its lack of inter-

est in the material elements that compose that form, the physical instantiations of play. By focusing on toys, I want to overcome that problem and describe how play can be effectively materialized in objects that are not formalized play but can be used in formalized play.

15. By this I mean that a toy is just a collection of signifiers, affordances and constraints placed to cue certain types of play behaviors. The meaning of the toy cannot be located in its design but in the way it is used, or in how the design is actualized in the act of playing with it.

16. Or, as Sutton-Smith (1986) would put it, a toy is an instrument for the different rhetorics of play. See also Suits (2005) for a reflection on different types of play and what is required to engage in play activities, particularly the idea of games as creating unnecessary challenges.

17. In this sense, I follow Benjamin's footsteps, claiming that the freedom afforded by some toys is better because it leads to the positive aspects of play: "Because the more appealing toys are, in the ordinary sense of the term, the further they are from genuine playthings; the more they are based on imitation, the further away they lead us from real, living play" (Benjamin 1999b, 115–116).

18. Sutton-Smith (1986): "The toy is a model of the kind of isolation that is essential to progress in the modern world. Just as it, as a miniature, is abstracted from the world about it, which it represents in some way, so must growing persons learn to abstract themselves from the world around" (24).

19. This material thinking is relatively close to Heidegger's ideas on technology, particularly those expressed in "The Question Concerning Technology" (available at http://www.wright.edu/cola/Dept/PHL/Class/P.Internet/PITexts/QCT.html, accessed December 12, 2011).

20. "To be sure, play is always liberating. Surrounded by a world of giants, children use play to create a world appropriate to their size. But the adult, who finds himself threatened by the real world and can find no escape, removes its sting by playing with its image in reduced form" (Benjamin 1999b, 100).

21. The idea of dimensions is an interpretation of Lim, Stolterman, and Tenenberg's (2008) nomenclature to describe prototypes. In this sense, I believe that toys are excellent ways of thinking about prototyping for games, particularly for digital games, since they can be described using prototyping theory. In other words, for prototyping games, toys provide a natural way of starting to explore different design spaces.

22. I am referring here to the fact that games are not the only or even the dominant form of play and that toys and their materiality are as important as any other form of play for understanding playing.

23. http://www.generativemusic.com/ (accessed December 12, 2011).

24. Affordances, signifiers, and constraints are part of the design process, that is, they are consciously built in. Filters might be consciously created, but they might also be "discovered" by players as they interact with an object with a playful attitude. I am trying to stay away here from a normative design stance because I believe that in the design of games and toys, the question of how the object filters the activity is a productive one to ask during conceptualization.

25. That has an effect in professional sports. In every Soccer World Cup, a new ball is presented, each time a more perfect sphere than in the past. And in every World Cup, some players complain that the new ball "plays differently" than the previous ones did, affecting their game.

26. http://vectorpark.com/levers/ (accessed December 12, 2011).

27. As I noted in chapter 1, this book proposes a romantic vision of play, one driven by Schiller's (1988) famous statement that people are fully human only in play. I addressed the problems with my approach to play in the introduction and return to them in the conclusion to this book in chapter 8.

Chapter 4

1. I am referring here to the Santa Maria and Easter Islands playground: http://monstrum.dk/projekter/santa-maria-og-paaskeoeerne-paa-aarhus-plads.

2. Monstrum.dk.

3. The adventure playground was the idea of Carl Theodor Sørensen, even though the modern understanding of the word comes from the British adoption of his ideas, thanks to the initiative of Lady Allen of Hurtwood. Kozlovsky (2008) provides an excellent critical history of the adventure playground.

4. Solomon (2005) gives a compelling account of the trivialization of the American playground and modern attempts to revitalize these spaces as creative social spaces.

5. See, for instance, Seitinger et al.(2006), Lentini and Decortis (2010), or Wilhemsson (2006).

6. Academically, a good starting reference is Soute, Markopoulos, and Magielse (2010). I also recommend that readers look at playground designers like PlayAlive (http://www.playalive.dk/Globalt/produkt.htm) or Creative Playthings (http://www.creativeplaythings.com). These types of playgrounds are enhanced by technology, but that technology is used to monitor and closely steer behaviors within the playground. Therefore, they are examples of a tendency toward more regulated, normative play in the context of the otherwise more open spaces of the classic playground.

7. Note that the adventure playground is a pattern in Alexander et al.'s *A Pattern Language* (1977, nr. 73).

8. Kozlovsky (2008) suggests this critical reading of playground design, comparing it to panopticist designs.

9. A good example, besides the Monstrum playground, is Berlin's MountMitte playground, oriented to an adult experience of vertigo. See http://mountmitte.de (accessed February 5, 2013).

10. But not exclusively so. Even an architect like Alexander writes in *A Pattern Language*, "Any kind of playground which disturbs, or reduces, the role of imagination and makes the child more passive, more the recipient of someone else's imagination, may look nice, may be clean, may be sage, may be healthy—but it just cannot satisfy the fundamental need which play is all about" (1977, 368).

11. Again, Solomon (2005) provides an excellent overview of the American example, in which overtly protective safety regulations made playgrounds boring spaces for children.

12. Dumas and Laforest (2008) give a good account of skateboarding and its relation to urban spaces and sports.

13. The literature on parkour and space is quite varied. For a deeper version of the analysis of the relations between urbanism and parkour, I recommend O'Grady (2012), Geyh (2006), Mould (2009), Bavinton (2007), Rawlinson and Guaralda (2011), and Waern, Balan, and Nevelsteen (2012).

14. See Nitsche (2009) for a comprehensive account of the relation between space and games.

15. Interestingly, Vincent Ocasla, a player of *Sim City 2000*, claims that this game can be "finished" and shows as proof Magnasanti, a totalitarian city of 6 million digital inhabitants. See http://www.youtube.com/watch?v=NTJQTc-TqpU and http://www.vice.com/read/the-totalitarian-buddhist-who-beat-sim-city.

16. See visitproteus.com. Incidentally, on its release on January 30, 2013, *Proteus* created some stir in the gaming communities because it does not fit the traditional, conservative definitions of games. For me, *Proteus* is an object we play with and a space we play in, and so it can be defined as a game—as well as a playground or even a toy. What is important is not its ontological nature but what we do with it.

Chapter 5

1. Art and aesthetics, as I will note throughout the chapter, are not the same thing, but as Danto (2009) wrote, "Ontologically, aesthetics is not essential to art—but rhetorically, it is central. The artist uses aesthetics to transform or confirm attitudes. That is not the same as putting us in the mood of calm aesthetic contemplations, which has tended to hijack the concept of aesthetics" (116). See also Jansen, O'Connor, and Halsall (2009).

2. Interestingly, the history of the novel is one that started with playful forms, like *Don Quixote* and *Tristram Shandy*; only in the nineteenth century did it become a more serious affair. Are games and toys, so often forced to be "serious" to be respected, following the same path? And if so, what are we losing?

3. The relation of play and the twentieth-century avant-garde, particularly with the Fluxus and situationist international moments, is particularly interesting. Flanagan (2009) is the reference text for this history, though Friedman (1998) and Knabb (2007) are also extremely interesting.

4. See, for instance, Stiles's (2007) reflections on Fluxus, play, and humor: "Filled with the marvel of a sense of discovery and release, Fluxus humor escorts freedoms: the freedom to play and goof-off, the freedom to value that play as an aesthetic habit (one's brand), the freedom to abandon reason and aesthetics and just to be" (57).

5. Again Stiles (2007), writing about Fluxus, summarizes this idea more precisely: "In order to really goof-off well, the instrumental sense of purpose deeply ingrained in Western ego and epistemology has to be abandoned" (52).

6. I think that the beauty of play also says something about art and the works of art, an idea I owe to Dave Hickey (2007): "What if works of art were considered to be what they actually are—frivolous objects or entities with no intrinsic value that only acquire value through a complex process of socialization during which some are empowered by an ongoing sequence of private, mercantile, journalistic, and institutional investments that are irrevocably extrinsic to them and to any intention they might embody" (119).

7. The most interesting recent summary of this relation can be found in Kwastek (2013). She addresses many of the problems that arise when using classic play theories in the study of the arts, particularly digital aesthetics. Kwastek acknowledges that play is a fundamental concept for understanding the aesthetics of interactive digital art. Her chapter on the aesthetics of play is good to read in parallel with this book, as I have

tried to solve some of the interpretational problems she observes in her study.

8. See, for instance, Gumbrecht (2006): "What we enjoy in the great moments of a ballgame is not just the goal, the touchdown, the home run, or the slam-dunk. It is the beautiful individual play that takes form prior to the score.... A form is any phenomenon with the capacity of presenting itself to our sense and experience in clear distinction from everything that is not a part of it. But a beautiful play is more than just a form—it is an epiphany of form. A beautiful play is produced by the sudden, surprising convergence of several athletes' bodies in time and space" (189–190).

9. Drucker (2009) presents an interesting view on the relationship between aesthetics and computation: "The role of aesthetics is to illuminate the ways in which the forms of knowledge provoke interpretation. Insofar as the formal logic of computational environments validates instrumental applications regarding the management and creation of digital artifacts, imaginative play is crucial to keeping that logic from asserting a totalizing authority on knowledge and its forms. Aesthesis, I suggest, allows us to insist on the value of subjectivity that is central to aesthetic artifacts—works of art in the traditional sense—and to place the subjectivity at the core of knowledge production" (xiii).

10. Bourriaud (2002).

11. Kester (2004, 2011).

12. C. Bishop (2004, 2009, 2012).

13. Kaprow (2003).

14. Of course, it is not an instant but the appreciation of the process that matters, that makes play beautiful: "Scoring serves to define and articulate *overcoming opposition*. It helps determine the completeness of play and thereby the overall form of the game. It gives a closure to our experience of sport often lacking in everyday life.... To appreciate the conclusion, though, we must see it as the fulfillment of what has preceded" (Kupfer, 1988, 462–463).

15. Even Sartre (1988) would agree: "But there is always in sport an appropriative component. In reality sport is a free transformation of the worldly environment into the supporting element of the action. This fact makes it creative like art" (170).

16. However, there are always ethical issues when winning is seen as the goal. See Hardman et al. (1996), or Feezell (2006).

17. In this sense, I am closer to Adorno's ideas that play and art, at least the high kind of art, modernist expression, that Adorno (2004) privileged, might be at odds with each other: "In art, play is from the outset disciplinary; it fulfills the taboo on expression that inheres in the ritual of imitation; when art exclusively plays, nothing remains of expression" (400).

18. See http://doougle.net/projects/mega-girp.html (accessed February 6, 2013).

19. This is not to say that the objects are not important. They are, but mostly as facilitators of the experience of play, as elements in the ecology of play: "Aesthetic objects create a space for reflection, through experience. They break the unity of object as product and thing as self-identical that are the hallmarks of a consumerist culture. They do this through their conceptual structure and execution, in the play between idea and expression. An aesthetic object may be simple or complex, but it inserts itself into a historical continuum of ideas in such a way as to register. Aesthetic objects make an argument about the nature of art as expression and experience. They perform that argument about what art is and can be, and what can be expressed and in what ways, at any given moment" (Drucker, 2009, 180).

20. See Bourriaud (2002) but also, and a more poignant work, Youngman (2011).

21. For instance: "The first question we should ask ourselves when looking at a work of art is: —Does it give me the chance to exist in front of it, or, on the contrary, does it deny me as a subject, refusing to consider the Other in its structure? Does the space-time factor suggested or described by this work, together with the laws governing it, tally with

my aspirations in real life? Does it criticize what is deemed to be criticizable? Could I live in a space-time structure corresponding to this reality?" (Bourriaud 2002, 57).

22. A description of it can be found at http://www.moma.org/collection/object.php?object_id=147206 (accessed February 6, 2013).

23. http://fingleforipad.com.

24. The origins and history of the game Ninja are obscure. A canonical description of the rules can be found here: http://ultimateninjacombat.com (accessed February 6, 2013).

25. http://www.precise-ambiguities.net (accessed February 6, 2013).

26. This is best summarized by C. Bishop (2004)—for example: "In the meantime it is necessary to observe that it is only a short step from regarding the *image* as a social relationship to Bourriaud's argument that the *structure* of an art work produces a social relationship. However, identifying what the structure of a relational art work *is* is no easy task, precisely because the work claims to be open-ended. This problem is exacerbated by the fact that relational art works are an outgrowth of installation art, a form that has from its inception solicited the literal presence of the viewer" (63).

27. Again, Bishop (2004) writes: "If relational aesthetics requires a unified subject as a pre- requisite for community-as-togetherness, then Hirschhorn and Sierra provide a mode of artistic experience more adequate to the divided and incomplete subject of today. This relational antagonism would be predicated not on social harmony, but on exposing that which is repressed in sustaining the semblance of this harmony. It would thereby provide a more concrete and polemical grounds for rethinking our relationship to the world and to one other" (79).

28. In Kester's (2004) own description of his theory: "The emphasis is on the character of this interaction, not the physical or formal integrity of a given artifact or the artist's experience in producing it. The object-based artwork (with some exceptions) is produced entirely by the artist and only subsequently offered to the viewer. As a result, the viewer's response has no immediate reciprocal effect on the constitution of the

work. Further, the physical object remains essentially static. Dialogical projects, in contrast, unfold through a process of performative interaction" (10).

29. Though context is extremely important, it is so in the perspective of what Kester (2004) calls the catalyzation of the viewer: "This catalyzation of the viewer, the movement toward direct interaction, decisively shifts the locus of aesthetic meaning from the moment of creative plenitude in the solitary act of making (or the viewer's imaginative reconstruction of this act) to a social and discursive realm of shared experience, dialogue, and physical movement" (54).

30. "What is at stake in these projects is not dialogue per se but the extent to which the artist is able to catalyze emancipatory insights *through* dialogue" (C. Kester, 2004, 69).

31. See Wilson and Sicart (2010) for a brief introduction to abusive games.

32. The classic monograph on Nordic live action role playing games is Stenros and Montola (2011).

33. Jeepen games are an experimental type of role-playing game extremely close to improvisational theater: a scenario is laid out for players, who through mostly improvised interactions explore a topic rather than a narrative—though the experience can be based on a narrative. See http://jeepen.org.

34. http://jeepen.org/games/fatmandown/.

35. For a proper description of the concept of bleed, see Waern (2011).

36. "Play, of course, is at the heart of experimentation. Elsewhere, I've pointed out the crucial difference in the English language between playing and gaming. Gaming involves winning or losing a desired goal. Playing is open-ended and, potentially, everybody 'wins'. Playing has no stated purpose other than more playing. It is usually not serious in content or attitude, whereas gaming, which can also involve playing if it is subordinated to winning, is at heart competitive" (Kaprow, 2003, 250).

37. "Avant-garde lifelike art is not nearly as serious as avant-garde art-like art. Often it is quite humorous. It isn't very interested in the great Western tradition, either, since it tends to mix things up: body with mind, individual with people in general, civilization with nature, and so on. Thus it mixes up the traditional art genres or avoids them entirely.... Lifelike art makers' principal dialogue is not with art but with everything else, one event suggesting another. If you don't know much about life, you'll miss much of the meaning of the lifelike art that's born of it. Indeed, it is never certain if an artist who creates avant-garde lifelike art is an artist" (Kaprow, 2003, 203).

38. Originally designed for a Penn and Teller's never-published game (see http://en.wikipedia.org/wiki/Penn_%26_Teller's_Smoke_and _Mirrors), *Desert Bus* has seen its popularity grow thanks to its quirkiness and charm. A playable version of the game can be found at http:// desertbus-game.org.

39. A classic example of the extreme interpretation of this idea is Pain-Station: http://www.painstation.de.

40. "As direct play is denied to adults and gradually discouraged in children, the impulse to play emerges not in true games alone, but in unstated ones of power and deception; people find themselves playing less with each other than on or off each other" (Kaprow, 2003, 121).

41. Interestingly, Adorno (2004) might have agreed with this idea: "Only when play becomes aware of its own terror, as in Beckett, does it in any way share in art's power of reconciliation" (400).

42. A valid approach to the aesthetics of playful objects might be taken from a Gadamerian perspective, like Davey (2009): "The brilliance of an artwork's speculative revelation is that it can enable us to perceive a circle of meaning where prior to the insight we saw none. The shock of aesthetic or speculative recognition is suddenly seeing events and experiences that we assumed to be a disparate and unconnected as being in fact connected and moving toward a fulfillment of meaning that we had not anticipated" (151).

43. I would also like plaything designers to take up this challenge and allow rowdier and more dangerous and shocking approaches to making people play, like the coordinated melees that can happen when playing *B.U.T.T.O.N.* As Hickey (2007) wrote: "I would like some bad-acting and wrong-thinking. I would like to see some art that is courageously silly and frivolous, that cannot be construed as anything else. I would like a bunch of twenty-three-year-old troublemakers to become so enthusiastic, so noisy, and so involved in some stupid, seductive, destructive brand of visual culture that I would feel called upon to rise up in righteous indignation, spewing vitriol, to bemoan the arrogance and self-indulgence of the younger generation and all of its artifacts" (123).

Chapter 6

1. With his gesture when receiving the 1968 Olympic Gold Medal for the 200 meter dash, Tommie Smith brought the world's attention to the African American black power movement. Jesse Owens defeated the Nazi athletes in the Berlin Olympics of 1936 while retaining sportsmanship in his treatment to the competitors. Diego Armando Maradona became first a symbol of overcoming poverty through talent and then a political symbol when he almost singlehandedly eliminated England in the 1986 Soccer World Cup. Martina Navratilova, perhaps the best tennis player ever, has used her worldwide fame to speak out on gay rights and political issues.

2. Videos of the goals scored in that match can be found here: http://www.youtube.com/watch?v=KY40__rBvSk (accessed February 2, 2013).

3. The conflict between the United Kingdom and Argentina over the sovereignty of the Falklands was historically long, though the Argentine dictatorship in power between 1976 and 1983 saw it as an opportunity for diverting attention from the country's catastrophic economic situation. The Argentinian defeat in the war had the positive outcome of accelerating the effects on the decline of the military junta.

4. See Adorno (2001), particularly the essay "Free Time."

5. In his reading of Marx, Henricks (2006) hints at this political interpretation. A selection of relevant articles on this topic can be found in Morgan and Meier (1988).

6. The works of Boal (2002, 2008) and Freire (1996, 2001, 2010).

7. The history of critical and political play has been dominated by a perspective centered in the rich Northern Hemisphere countries, which means that we have ignored the importance of play as a critical device in the poverty and dictatorship-rammed countries of Latin America. I am indebted to Enric Llagostera for this observation.

8. This is particularly the case of Freire's *Pedagogy of the Oppressed* (1996), fundamental to understanding the liberating powers of performance.

9. See Stenros and Montola (2011). Notice, however, that Nordic live action role playing games, while examples of critical play, have very different sociocultural and economic contexts from the Marxist Latin American theories mentioned before.

10. Munthe-Kaas (2011) describes the dystopian *System Danmarc* Nordic live action role playing games, which presented the idea of a futuristic Danish state in which the underclass was confined to ghettos and deprived of any rights or welfare state benefits.

11. Virtanen and Jokinen (2011) describes the Nordic live action role playing game *Ground Zero*, which explores the "first day of a nuclear holocaust" (65).

12. See Debord and Wolman (2009), or Knabb (2007) for an account of the politics of the Situationist International. Wark (2011) provides an appropriate sociocultural overview.

13. The work of culture jammers *Adbusters* is clearly influenced by Debord's theories, though it is always complicated to delimit how much in *Adbusters* is politics, and how much is a pose. Go to https://www.adbusters.org and draw your own conclusion.

14. Richter and Britt (1997) give a good overview of the politics of Dada in the context of the art world and the political situation of the early twentieth century.

15. Friedman (1998) is the canonical Fluxus reference.

16. Bogost (2007) has a more nuanced and detailed approach to the problem of political or persuasive games, and how technology plays an important, material role in their configuration. However, Bogost is still focused on the object itself rather than the experience or performance. Another example in this tradition would be Frasca (2004).

17. That is, play can be the performance of political ideas for expression or for exploration, as Boal (2008) and Freire (1996) suggested.

18. This 2009 *Guardian* article explains kettling and its implications: http://www.guardian.co.uk/world/2009/apr/03/g20-protests-police -tactics (accessed February 7, 2012).

19. Metakettle is actually a political game that has never been played, since the developers never found the occasion to do so. However, the game rules and designer notes are clear enough to give an idea of the game as it should be played: http://www.terrorbullgames.co.uk/games/ metakettle_pnpgame.php.

20. Because of its focus on humor: "In a society thoroughly indoctrinated with prescribed cultural values, the idea of affirming personal idiosyncrasies that could include goofing-off, seems irresponsible and ridiculous—but liberating" (Stiles 2007, 53).

21. In this sense, play is connected to the notion of art that Kaprow (2003) defends: "Power in art is not like that in a nation or in big business. A picture never changed the price of eggs. But a picture can change our dreams; and pictures may in time clarify our values. The power of artists is precisely the influence they world over the fantasies of their public.... As it is involved in quality, art is a moral act" (53).

22. This is similar to what Freire (1996) criticizes as the banking model of education, where students are there to be filled with knowledge by the teacher.

23. The importance of performativity in the mundane was already highlighted by Schechner (1988): "Work and other daily activities con-

tinuously feed on the underlying ground of playing, using the play mood for refreshment, energy, unusual ways of turning this around, insights, breaks, opening and, especially, *looseness*.... Looseness encourages the discovery of new configurations and twists of ideas and experiences" (17).

24. The canonical and brilliant critical history of hacktivism in modern days is Coleman (2012).

25. The *New York Times* ran a comprehensive story on trolling in 2008: http://www.nytimes.com/2008/08/03/magazine/03trolls-t.html?_r =1&pagewanted=1.

26. http://www.4chan.org

27. More details on the importance of the silly humor in these online sites can be found here: http://canopycanopycanopy.com/15/our _weirdness_is_free.

28. This was the so-called project chanology. See https://encyclopedia dramatica.se/PROJECT_CHANOLOGY.

29. Some relevant academic reflections on trolling and politics are Coleman (2011), Knuttila (2011), and Vichot (2009). Another interesting reference is http://www.youtube.com/watch?v=oHg5SJYRHA0.

30. http://en.wikipedia.org/wiki/Never_Gonna_Give_You_Up.

31. In this sense, it is close to Schechner's idea of dark play: "Dark Play occurs when contradictory realities coexist, each seemingly capable of cancelling the other out" (12).

32. See Savicic and Savic (2012).

33. See http://michaelrakowitz.com/projects/parasite/ (accessed October 17, 2013). See also similar projects at http://unpleasant.pravi.me/ category/strategies/reapropriation/ (accessed October 17, 2013).

34. See http://criticalengineering.org.

35. http://newstweek.com.

Chapter 7

1. The idea of games being a form of play is derived from the common idea that games are ontologically defined by their rules. Good examples of this argument are Salen and Zimmerman (2004), Suits (2005), and Kirkpatrick (2011).

2. The discussion on how the form of games can evolve through time is not well discussed in the game studies literature, even though Juul (2007) explored this topic in his history of tile matching games.

3. UEFA is a famously conservative institution that tries to keep the practice of professional soccer as low tech as possible. See J. Wilson (2008) for a parallel history of the evolution of game tactics and of game rules.

4. The North American Scrabble Players Association maintains a web page with the official rules of competitive Scrabble: http://www .scrabbleplayers.org/w/Welcome_to_NASPAWiki (accessed October 29, 2013).

5. I find Simon's (1996) reflections on the nature of an artifact a good illustration of this idea: "An artifact can be thought of as a meeting point—an 'interface' in today's terms—between an 'inner' environment, the substance and organization of the artifact itself, and an 'outer' environment, the surroundings in which it operates" (6).

6. A symptom of this is the rising popularity of game design programs in universities around the world. However, the profession of the game designer still has to find its place in the popular culture collective mind: there are virtually no game designers represented in sit-coms, Hollywood movies, or pulp novels.

7. Johan Huizinga and Roger Caillois, the founding fathers of game studies in the twentieth century, gave games a privileged position in their understanding of play, even though they also mentioned rituals and other communitarian activities as important. In fact, it is sociologists like Erving Goffman and critical thinkers like Paul Freire and Augusto Boal who focused on play more than on games.

8. By "games" here, I am referring mostly to computer games, which are now a dominant economic and expressive cultural power. A very interesting argument about the cultural importance of games, without resorting to trite economic arguments, was put forth by Anthropy (2012): more and more people are using games to express themselves, just as they do with music and poetry.

9. For instance, the revitalization of playgrounds as public spaces for play or the popularity of software toys in smart phone platforms.

10. With German romanticism, an era in which the original creator was privileged was started; we are still in this era, a reflection of the importance we assign to creators of original material.

11. A good example of this is the inclusion in the 2011 New York Museum of Modern Art exhibition Talk to Me of video and computer games: http://www.moma.org/interactives/exhibitions/2011/talktome/. See also Antonelli (2011).

12. See for instance Bogost (2007, 2011), Flanagan (2009), Frasca (2007), and Fullerton (2008).

13. Interestingly enough, in design research even the most formalist and functionalist arguments show awareness of the importance of context and use: "Product semantics as a study of the symbolic qualities of man-made forms in the cognitive and social contexts of their use and the application of the knowledge gained to objects of industrial design" (Krippendorf, 1995, 157), and, "Meaning is a cognitively constructed relationship. It selectively connects features of an object and features of its (real environment or imagined) context into a coherent unity" (159).

14. See Cross (2007)—for example: "Designing is a process of pattern synthesis, rather than pattern recognition.... This pattern-constructing feature has been recognized as lying at the core of design activity by Alexander in his 'constructive diagrams' and 'pattern language'. The designer learns to think in this sketch-like form, in which the abstract patterns of user requirements are turned into the concrete patterns of an actual object" (24–25).

15. See, for example, Pye (1978): "The designer can only ensure that the intended results do occur, by selecting certain properties for its components, namely those required by the nature of the result, of the objects, and of the energy put on it. That in principle is his job" (19).

16. Löwgren and Stolterman (2004) make a sympathetic case for the thoughtful interaction designer as a creator aware of the morals and politics involved in her work.

17. A classic work on the aesthetics of design is Pye (1978). See also Drucker (2009), Hallnäs and Redström (2002), and Hekkert (2006).

18. In the words of Stolterman and Löwgren (2004), design is about "*tight coupling*.... Minimize the distance between user intentions, user actions, and the effects of these actions" (118).

19. I am using the term as defined by Norman (2004).

20. The idea of games as putting unnecessary obstacles as challenges is inherited from Suits (2005).

Chapter 8

1. See Lemon Joust: http://www.deepfun.com/fun/2012/07/lemon-jousting/ (accessed February 11, 2013).

2. http://www.ideotoylab.com/balloonimals.html.

3. This is a simplified understanding of computation and computers, which are also capable of helping to send people to the moon or allow Facebook to exist.

4. Norbert Wiener is probably the most interesting philosopher in the classic discipline of cybernetics, a type of system theory. His classic book, *The Human Use of Human Beings* (1988), provides a deeply humanistic, ethics-driven account of systems theory and its importance for understanding human.

5. See tinysubversions.com. An updated list of Darius Kazemi's bots can be found here: https://twitter.com/tinysubversions/darius-kazemi-s-bots/members (accessed October 17, 2013).

6. https://twitter.com/AmIRiteBot (accessed October 17, 2013).

7. Other excellent Twitter bots are Metaphor-A-Minute (https://twitter.com/metaphorminute), Six Words Sale (https://twitter.com/SixWordSale), and Two Headlines (https://twitter.com/TwoHeadlines) (accessed October 17, 2013).

8. This is an idea inspired by Bogost (2012) and Latour (2013).

9. The work of Dourish (2001) has been particularly influential in my way of seeing technologies as stage-setters and props for performance.

10. And again, this is an argument that should be read in the context of my romantic theory of play. It can be argued that the combination of play and computation is exciting when it carefully balances the human being in the world and the computational being in the world—when the human and the thing both play expressively.

11. Or humanistic: a cultural expression of being human and human beings.

12. Computation need not be human to be a form of expression or of being in the world. I am taking an anthropocentric, and therefore sometimes philosophically outdated, perspective here, but I don't want to imply that computational play is not expressive, productive, or ontologically relevant.

References

Adorno, Theodor. 2001. *The Culture Industry*. 2nd ed. New York: Routledge.

Adorno, Theodor. 2004. *Aesthetic Theory*. New York: Continuum.

Adorno, Theodor, and Max Horkheimer. 2010. *The Dialectic of Enlightenment*. New York: Verso.

Alexander, Christopher, Sara Ishikawa, Murray Silverstein, Max Jacobson, Ingrid Fiksdahl-King, and Shlomo Angel. 1977. *A Pattern Language: Towns, Buildings, Construction*. Oxford: Oxford University Press.

Anthropy, Anna. 2012. *Rise of the Videogame Zinesters: How Freaks, Normals, Amateurs, Artists, Dreamers, Drop-Outs, Queers, Housewives, and People Like You Are Taking Back an Art Form*. New York: Seven Stories Press.

Antonelli, Paola. 2011. *Talk to Me*. New York: MoMA.

Avedon, Elliot M., and Brian Sutton-Smith. 1971. The Structural Elements of Games. In *The Study of Games*. New York: Wiley.

Bakhtin, Mikhail. 1984. *Rabelais and His World*. Bloomington: Indiana University Press.

Bakhtin, Mikhail M. 2008. *The Dialogic Imagination*, edited by Michael Holquist and translated by Caryl Emerson. Austin: University of Texas Press.

Bavinton, N. 2007. From Obstacle to Opportunity: Parkour, Leisure, and the Reinterpretation of Constraints. *Annals of leisure research* 10, no. 3-4: 391–412.

Benjamin, Walter. 1999a. Old Toys. In *Selected Writings*, vol. 2: 1927–1930, edited by Michael W. Jennings, Howard Eiland, and Gary Smith. Cambridge, MA: Harvard University Press.

Benjamin, Walter. 1999b. The Cultural History of Toys. In *Selected Writings*, vol. 2: 1927–1930, edited by Michael W. Jennings, Howard Eiland, and Gary Smith. Cambridge, MA: Harvard University Press.

Benjamin, Walter. 1999c. Toys and Play. In *Selected Writings*, vol. 2: 1927–1930, edited by Michael W. Jennings, Howard Eiland, and Gary Smith. Cambridge, MA: Harvard University Press.

Benjamin, Walter. 1999d. *Selected Writings*, edited by Howard Eiland, Michael W. Jennings, and Gary Smith, 1927–1930. Cambridge, MA: Harvard University Press.

Bishop, Claire. 2004. Antagonism and Relational Aesthetics. *October*, Nr. 110: 51–79.

Bishop, Claire. 2009. The Social Turn: Collaboration and Its Discontents. In *Rediscovering Aesthetics*, edited by Francis Halsall, Julia Jensen, and Tony O'Connor. Stanford, CA: Stanford University Press.

Bishop, Claire. 2012. *Artificial Hells: Participatory Art and the Politics of Spectatorship*. London: Verso.

Blijlevens, Janneke, Marielle E.H. Creusen, and Jan P.L. Schoormans. 2009. How consumers perceive product appearance: The identification of three product appearance attributes. *International Journal of Design* 3 (3):27–35.

Boal, Augusto. 2002. *Games for Actors and Non-Actors*, 2nd ed. London: Routledge.

Boal, Augusto. 2008. *Theatre of the Oppressed*. London: Pluto Press.

Bogost, Ian. 2007. *Persuasive Games: The Expressive Power of Videogames*. Cambridge, MA: MIT Press.

Bogost, Ian, and Nick Montfort. 2009. *Racing the Beam. The Atari Video Computer System*. Cambridge, MA: MIT Press.

Bogost, Ian. 2011. *How to Do Things with Videogames*. Minneapolis: University of Minnesota Press.

Bogost, Ian. 2012. *Alien Phenomenology*. Open Humanities Press.

Bourriaud, Nicolas. 2002. *Relational Aesthetics*. Monts, France: Les Presses du Réel.

Brown, John Seely, and Paul Duguid. 1994. Borderline Issues: Social and Material Aspects of Design. *Human-Computer Interaction* 9 (1): 3–36.

Caillois, Roger. 2001. *Man, Play and Games*. Urbana: University of Illinois Press.

Coleman, G. 2011. *Anonymous: From the Lulz to Collective Action. The New Everyday: A Media Commons Project, 6*. Retrieved from Google Scholar.

Coleman, Gabriella. 2012. *Coding Freedom: The Ethics and Aesthetics of Hacking*. Princeton, NJ: Princeton University Press.

Consalvo, Mia. 2009. There Is No Magic Circle. *Games and Culture* 4 (4): 408–417.

Cross, Nigel. 2007. *Designerly Ways of Knowing*. Basel, Switzerland: Birkhäuser.

Danto, Arthur C. 2009. The Future of Aesthetics. In *Rediscovering Aesthetics*, edited by Francis Halsall, Julia Jansen, and Tony O'Connor. Stanford, CA: Stanford University Press.

Davey, Nicholas. 2009. Gadamer and the Ambiguity of Appearance. In *Rediscovering Aesthetics*, edited by Francis Halsall, Julia Jansen, and Tony O'Connor. Stanford, CA: Stanford University Press.

Debord, Guy, and Gil J. Wolman. 2009. Directions for the Use of Détournement. In *Documents of Contemporary Art: Appropriation*, edited by David Evans, 35–39. Cambridge, MA: MIT Press.

DeKoven, Bernie. 2002. *The Well-Played Game: A Playful Path to Whole-ness*. Lincoln, NE: Writers Club Press.

Deterding, Sebastian, Dan Dixon, Rilla Khaled, and Leonard Nacke. 2011a. From Game Design Elements to Gamefulness: Defining "Gamifi-cation". *MindTrek 2011 Proceedings*.

Deterding, Sebastian, Rilla Khaled, Leonard Nacke, and Dan Dixon. 2011b. Gamification: Toward a Definition. *CHI 2011 Workshop paper*.

Dourish, Paul. 2001. *Where the Action Is: The Foundations of Embodied Interaction*. Cambridge, MA: MIT Press.

Dourish, Paul. 2004. What We Talk about When We Talk about Con-text. *Personal and Ubiquitous Computing* 8 (1): 19–39.

Dreyfuss, Henry. 2003. *Designing for People*. New York: Allworth Press.

Drucker, Johanna. 2009. *Speclab: Digital Aesthetics and Projects in Specula-tive Computing*. Chicago: University of Chicago Press.

Dumas, Alex, and Sophie Laforest. 2008. "Intergenerational Conflict: What Can Skateboarding Tell Us About the Struggles for Legitimacy in the Field of Sports?" September 4. http://www.idrottsforum.org/articles/dumas-laforest/dumas-laforest080409.pdf.

Dunne, Anthony. 2006. *Hertzian Tales: Electronic Products, Aesthetic Expe-rience, and Critical Design*. Cambridge, MA: MIT Press.

Esposito, Joseph L. 1988. Play and Possibility. In *Philosophic Inquiry in Sport*, edited by William J. Morgan and Klaus V. Meier. Champaign, IL: Human Kinetics.

Feezell, R. 2006. *Sport, Play, and Ethical Reflection*. Champaign: Univer-sity of Illinois Press.

Fink, Eugen. 1988. The Ontology of Play. In *Philosophic Inquiry in Sport*, edited by William J. Morgan and Klaus V. Meier. Champaign, IL: Human Kinetics.

Flanagan, Mary. 2009. *Critical Play: Radical Game Design*. Cambridge, MA: MIT Press.

Frasca, G. 2004. Videogames of the Oppressed: Critical Thinking, Education, Tolerance, and Other Trivial Issues. In *First Person: New Media as Story, Performance, and Game*, edited by Noah Wardrip-Fruin and Pat Harrigan, 85–94. Cambridge, MA: MIT Press.

Frasca, G. 2007. "Play the Message. Play, Game, and Videogame Rhetoric." PhD diss. IT University of Copenhagen. Retrieved from http://www.powerfulrobot.com/Frasca_Play_the_Message_PhD.pdf.

Freire, Paulo. 1996. *Pedagogy of the Oppressed*. London: Penguin.

Freire, Paulo. 2001. *Pedagogy of Freedom: Ethics, Democracy, and Civic Courage*. New York: Rowman & Littlefield.

Freire, Paulo. 2010. *Education for Critical Consciousness*. New York: Continuum.

Friedman, Ken. 1998. *The Fluxus Reader*. London: Academy Editions London.

Fullerton, Tracy. 2008. *Game Design Workshop: A Playcentric Approach to Creating Innovative Games*, 2nd ed. New York: Elsevier.

Gaver, William. 2009. Designing for Homo Ludens, Still. In *Re)Searching the Digital Bauhaus*, edited by Thomas Binder, Jonas Löwgren, and Lone Malmborg. London: Springer.

Gaver, William W, John Bowers, Andrew Boucher, Hans Gellerson, Sarah Pennington, Albrecht Schmidt, Anthony Steed, Nicholas Villars, *and* Brendan Walker. 2004. The Drift Table: Designing for Ludic Engagement. *In CHI '04 Extended Abstracts on Human Factors in Computing Systems*. New York: ACM Press.

Goffman, Erving. 1959. *The Presentation of the Self in Everyday Life*. New York: Anchor.

Goffman, Erving. 1961. *Encounters: Two Studies in the Sociology of Interaction*. Indianapolis: Bobbs-Merrill.

Goldblatt, David. 2006. *The Ball Is Round: A Global History of Soccer*. New York: Riverhead Books.

Grayson, Kent. 1999. The Opportunities and Dangers of Playful Consumption. In *Consumer Value: A Framework for Analysis and Research*, ed. Morris B. Holbrook. London, UK: Routledge.

Geyh, P. 2006. "Urban Free Flow: A Poetics of Parkour." *M/C Journal* 9, no. 3.

Gumbrecht, Hans Ulrich. 2006. *In Praise of Athletic Beauty*. Cambridge, MA: Harvard University Press.

Hallnäs, L., and J. Redström. 2002. From Use to Presence: On the Expressions and Aesthetics of Everyday Computational Things. *ACM Transactions on Computer-Human Interaction* 9 (2): 106–124.

Hallnäs, Lars, and Johan Redström. 2001. Slow Technology: Designing for Reflection. *Personal and Ubiquitous Computing* 5 (3): 201–212.

Halsall, Francis, Julia Jansen, and Tony O'Connor, eds. 2009. *Rediscovering Aesthetics: Transdisciplinary Voices from Art History, Philosophy, and Art Practice*. Stanford, CA: Stanford University Press.

Hardman, A., L. Fox, D. McLaughlin, and K. Zimmerman. 1996. On Sportsmanship and "Running Up the Score": Issues of Incompetence and Humiliation. *Journal of the Philosophy of Sport* 23 (1): 58–69.

Hekkert, Paul. 2006. Design Aesthetics: Principles of Pleasure in Design. *Psychological Science* 48 (2): 157–172.

Henricks, Thomas S. 2006. *Play Reconsidered: Sociological Perspectives on Human Expression*. Urbana: University of Illinois Press.

Henricks, Thomas S. 2009. Orderly and Disorderly Play: A Comparison. *American Journal of Play* 2: 12–40.

Hickey, Dave. 2007. Frivolity and Unction. In *The Artist's Joke*, ed. Jennifer Higgies. Cambridge, MA: MIT Press.

Holbrook, Morris B., and Elizabeth C. Hirschman. 1982. The Experiential Aspects of Consumption: Consumer Fantasies, Feelings, and Fun. *Journal of Consumer Research* 9 (2): 132–140.

Holbrook, Morris B., Robert W. Chestnutt, Terence A. Oliva, and Eric A. Greenleaf. 1984. Play as a Consumption Experience: The Roles of Emotions, Performance, and Personality in the Enjoyment of Games. *Journal of Consumer Research* 11 (2): 728–739.

Huizinga, Johan. 1992. *Homo Ludens: A Study of the Play-Element in Culture*. Boston: Beacon Press.

Isaacson, Walter. 2011. *Steve Jobs*. New York: Simon & Schuster.

Juul, Jesper. 2005. *Half-Real: Videogames between Real Rules and Fictional Worlds*. Cambridge, MA: MIT Press.

Juul, J. 2007. Swap Adjacent Gems to Make Sets of Three: A History of Matching Tile Games. *Artifact* 1 (4): 205–216.

Juul, Jesper. 2009. *A Casual Revolution*. Cambridge, MA: MIT Press.

Kaptelinin, Victor, and Bonnie A. Nardi. 2006. *Acting with Technology: Activity Theory and Interaction Design*. Cambridge, MA: MIT Press.

Kaprow, Alan. 2003. *Essays on the Blurring of Art and Life*. Berkeley: University of California Press.

Kester, Grant H. 2004. *Conversation Pieces: Community + Communication in Modern Art*. Berkeley: University of California Press.

Kester, Grant. 2011. *The One and the Many: Contemporary Collaborative Art in a Global Context*. Durham, NC: Duke University Press.

Kirkpatrick, Graeme. 2011. *Aesthetic Theory and the Video Game*. Manchester: Manchester University Press.

Kittler, Friedrich. 2010. *Optical Media*. Cambridge: Polity.

Knabb, Ken. 2007. *Situationist International Anthology*. London: Bureau of Public Secrets.

Knuttila, L. 2011. User Unknown: 4chan, Anonymity and Contingency. *First Monday* 16: 10–13.

Koster, Raph. 2005. *A Theory of Fun for Game Design*. Scottsdale, AZ: Paraglyph Press.

Kozlovsky, Roy. 2008. Adventure Playgrounds and Postwar Reconstruction. In *Designing* Modern Childhoods: History, Space, and the Material

Culture of Children, edited by Marta Gutman, Ning de Coninck-Smith, and Paula S. Fass, 171–190. New Jersey: Rutgers University Press.

Krippendorff, Klaus. 1995. On the Essential Contexts of Artifacts or on the Proposition That Design Is Making Sense (of Things). In *The Idea of Design: A Design Issues Reader*, edited by Victor Margolin and George R. Buchanan, 156–184. Cambridge, MA: MIT Press.

Kupfer, Joseph H. 1988. Sport—the Body Electric. In *Philosophic Inquiry in Sport*, edited by William J. Morgan and Klaus V. Meier. Champaign, IL: Human Kinetics.

Kwastek, Katja. 2013. *Aesthetics of Interaction in Digital Art*. Cambridge, MA: MIT Press.

Latour, Bruno. 1992. Where Are the Missing Masses? The Sociology of a Few Mundane Artifacts. In *Shaping Technology/Building Society*, edited by Wiebe Bijker and John Law. Cambridge, MA: MIT Press.

Latour, Bruno. 2005. *Reassembling the Social: An Introduction to Actor-Network-Theory*. Oxford: Oxford University Press.

Latour, Bruno. 2013. *An Inquiry into Modes of Existence*. Cambridge, MA: Harvard University Press.

Law, John, and John Hassard. 1999. *Actor Network Theory and After*. Oxford: Blackwell.

Lentini, Laura, and Françoise Decortis. 2010. Space and Places: When Interacting with and in Physical Space Becomes a Meaningful Experience. *Personal and Ubiquitous Computing* 14 (5): 407–415.

Lessig, Lawrence. 2000. *Code: And Other Laws of Cyberspace*. New York: Basic Books.

Lieberman, Josefa Nina. 1977. *Playfulness: Its Relationship to Imagination and Creativity*. New York: Academic Press New York.

Lim, Youn-Kyung, Erik Stolterman, and Josh Tenenberg. 2008. The Anatomy of Prototypes: Prototypes as Filters, Prototypes as Manifestations of Design Ideas. *ACM Transactions on Computer-Human Interaction* 15 (2): 1–27.

Meier, Klaus V. 1988. An Affair of Flutes: An Appreciation of Play. In *Philosophic Inquiry in Sport*, edited by William J. Morgan and Klaus V. Meier. Champaign, IL: Human Kinetics.

Molesworth, Mike, and Janice Denegri-Knott. 2008. The playfulness of eBay and the implications for business as a game-maker. *Journal of Macromarketing* 28 (4):369–380.

Mould, O. 2009. Parkour, the City, the Event. *Environment and Planning. D, Society & Space* 27 (4):738.

Morgan, William J., and Klaus V. Meier, eds. 1988. *Philosophic Inquiry in Sport*. Champaign, IL: Human Kinetics.

Munthe-Kaas, Peter. 2011. System Danmarc. In *Nordic LARP*, ed. Jaako Stenros and Markus Montola, 210–221. Stockholm: Fëa Livia.

Murray, Janet. 1998. *Hamlet on the Holodeck. The Future of Narrative in Cyberspace*. Cambridge, MA: The MIT Press.

Nam, Tek-Jin, and Changwon Kim. 2011. Design by Tangible Stories. *Enriching Interactive Everyday Products with Ludic Value International Journal of Design* 5 (1): 85–98.

Newton, Sidney. 2004. Designing as Disclosure. *Design Studies* 25 (1): 93–109.

Nietzsche, Friedrich. 1993. *The Birth of Tragedy*. London: Penguin.

Nitsche, Michael. 2008. *Video Game Spaces: Image, Play, and Structure in 3D Game Worlds*. Cambridge, MA: The MIT Press.

Norman, Donald. 2002. The Design of Everyday Things. New York: Basic Books.

Norman, Donald. 2004. *Emotional Design: Why We Love (or Hate) Everyday Things*. New York: Basic Books.

Norman, Donald. 2010. *Living with Complexity*. Cambridge, MA: MIT Press.

O'Grady, A. 2012. "Tracing the City—parkour Training, Play and the Practice of Collaborative Learning." *Theatre. Dance and Performance Training* 3 (2): 145–162.

Pye, David. 1978. *The Nature and Aesthetics of Design*. London: Barrie and Jenkins.

Rawlinson, C., and M. Guaralda. 2011. Play in the City: Parkour and Architecture. In *The First International Postgraduate Conference on Engineering, Designing and Developing the Built Environment for Sustainable Wellbeing*. Queensland University of Technology, April 27. Retrieved from http://eprints.qut.edu.au/42506/.

Richter, Hans. 1997. *Dada: Art and Anti-Art (World of Art)*. New York: Thames and Hudson.

Ritzer, George. 2000. *Sociological Theory*, 5th ed. New York: McGraw-Hill.

Salen, Katie, and Eric Zimmerman. 2004. *Rules of Play: Game Design Fundamentals*. Cambridge, MA: MIT Press.

Sartre, Jean-Paul. 1988. Play and Sport. In *Philosophic Inquiry in Sport*, edited by William J. Morgan and Klaus V. Meier. Champaign, IL: Human Kinetics.

Savicic, Gordan, and Selena Savic. 2012. *Unpleasant Design*. Rotterdam: Artist Edition.

Schechner, Richard. 1988. Playing. *Play and Culture* 1: 3–19.

Schechner, Richard. 2006. *Performance Studies: An Introduction*, 2nd ed. New York: Routledge.

Schmitz, Kenneth L. 1988. Sport and Play: Suspension of the Ordinary. In *Philosophic Inquiry in Sport*, edited by William J. Morgan and Klaus V. Meier. Champaign, IL: Human Kinetics.

Schüll, Natasha Döw. 2012. *Addiction by Design: Machine Gambling in Las Vegas*. Princeton, NJ: Princeton University Press.

Schwartz, Mattathias. 2008. "The Trolls among Us." *New York Times*, August 3.

Seitinger, S., E. Sylvan, O. Zuckerman, M. Popovic, and O. Zuckerman. 2006. "A New Playground Experience: Going Digital?" In *CHI'06 Extended Abstracts on Human Factors in Computing Systems*.

Sengers, Phoebe, Kirsten Boehner, Shay David, and Joseph Kaye. 2005. "Reflective Design." In *Proceedings of the 4th Decennial Conference on Critical Computing: Between Sense and Sensibility*, edited by Olav W. Bertelsen, Niels Olof Bouvin, Peter G. Krogh, and Morten Kyng, 49–58. ACM, New York, USA.

Sengers, Phoebe, and Bill Gaver. 2006. "Staying Open to Interpretation: Engaging Multiple Meanings in Design and Evaluation." In *Proceedings of the 6th Conference on Designing Interactive Systems*, 99–108. ACM, New York, USA.

Sicart, Miguel. 2011. Against Procedurality. *Game Studies* 11 (3). http://gamestudies.org/1103/articles/sicart_ap.

Simon, Herbert A. 1996. *The Sciences of the Artificial*. 3rd ed. Cambridge, MA: MIT Press.

Solomon, Susan G. 2005. *American Playgrounds: Revitalizing Community Space*. NH, Lebanon: University Press of New England.

Soute, Iris, Panos Markopoulos, and Remco Magielse. 2010. Head Up Games: Combining the Best of Both Worlds by Merging Traditional and Digital Play. *Personal and Ubiquitous Computing* 14 (5): 435–444.

Stenros, Jaako, and Markus Montola, eds. 2011. *Nordic LARP*. Stockholm: Fëa Livia.

Stewart, Susan. 1993. *On Longing: Narratives of the Miniature, the Gigantic, the Souvenir, the Collection*. Durham, NC: Duke University Press.

Stiles, Kristine. 2007. Fluxus Performance and Humour. *In The Artist's Joke, edited by Jennifer Higgies*. Cambridge, MA: MIT Press.

Stolterman, Erik, and Jonas Löwgren. 2004. *Thoughtful Interaction Design: A Design Perspective on Information Technology*. Cambridge, MA: MIT Press.

Suits, Bernard. 1988. Tricky Triad: Games, Play and Sport. In *Philosophic Inquiry in Sport*, edited by William J. Morgan and Klaus V. Meier. Champaign, IL: Human Kinetics.

Suits, Bernard. 2005. *The Grasshopper: Games, Life and Utopia*. Peterborough, Ontario: Broadview Press.

Sutton-Smith, Brian. 1986. *Toys as Culture*. New York: Gardner Press.

Sutton-Smith, Brian. 1997. *The Ambiguity of Play*. Cambridge, MA: Harvard University Press.

Taylor, T. L. 2006a. Does Wow Change Everything? How a Pvp Server, Multinational Playerbase, and Surveillance Mod Scene Caused Me Pause. *Games and Culture* 1 (4): 318–337.

Taylor, T. L. 2006b. *Play between Worlds: Exploring Online Game Culture*. Cambridge, MA: MIT Press.

Taylor, T. L. 2009. The Assemblage of Play. *Games and Culture* 4 (4): 331–339.

Turkle, Sherry, ed. 2007. *Evocative Objects: Things We Think With*. Cambridge, MA: MIT Press.

Verbeek, Peter Paul. 2006. *What Things Do: Philosophical Reflections on Technology, Agency, and Design*. University Park: Pennsylvania State University Press.

Vichot, Ray. 2009. *Doing It for the "Lulz": Online Communities of Practice and Offline Tactical Media*. Master's thesis, Georgia Institute of Technology. Retrieved from http://smartech.gatech.edu/bitstream/handle/1853/28098/vichot_ray_200905_mast.pdf?sequence=1.

Virtanen, Jori, and Jami Jokinen. 2011. Ground Zero. In *Nordic LARP*, edited by J. Stenros and M. Montola, 64–71. Stockholm: Fëa Livia.

von Schiller, Friedrich. 1988. Play and Beauty. In *Philosophic Inquiry in Sport*, edited by William J. Morgan and Klaus V. Meier. Champaign, IL: Human Kinetics.

Waern, Annika. 2011. "'I'm in Love with Someone That Doesn't Exist!!' Bleed in the Context of a Computer Game." In *Nordic Digra Proceedings*. http://www.digra.org/dl/db/10343.00215.pdf.

Waern, A., E. Balan, and K. Nevelsteen. 2012. Athletes and Street Acrobats: Designing for Play as a Community Value in Parkour." In *Proceed-*

ings of the 2012 ACM Annual Conference on Human Factors in Computing Systems.

Wardrip-Fruin, Noah. 2009. *Expressive Processing. Digital Fictions, Computer Games, and Software Studies.* Cambridge, MA: MIT Press.

Wark, McKenzie. 2011. *The Beach beneath the Street: The Everyday Life and Glorious Times of the Situationist International.* New York: Verso.

Wiener, Norbert. 1988. *The Human Use of Human Beings: Cybernetics and Society.* New York: Da Capo Press.

Wilhelmsson, Ulf. 2006. "Computer Games as Playground and Stage." In *Proceedings of the 2006 International Conference on Game Research and Development* (CyberGames '06), 62–68. Murdoch University, Australia.

Wilson, Douglas. 2011. Brutally Unfair Tactics Totally OK Now: On Self-Effacing Games and Unachievements. *Game Studies* 11 (1). http://gamestudies.org/1101/articles/wilson.

Wilson, Douglas, and Miguel Sicart. 2010. "Now It's Personal. On Abusive Game Design." In *Proceedings of the International Academic Conference on the Future of Game Design and Technology* (Futureplay '10), 40–47. ACM, New York, USA.

Wilson, Jonathan. 2008. *Inverting the Pyramid: A History of Football Tactics.* London: Orion Books.

Winner, Langdon. 1986. *The Whale and the Reactor: A Search for Limits in an Age of High Technology.* Chicago: University of Chicago Press.

Wittgenstein, Ludwig. 1991. *Philosophical Investigations.* Oxford: Wiley-Blackwell.

Wright, Peter, Jayne Wallace, and John McCarthy. 2008. Aesthetics and Experience-Centered Design. *ACM Transactions on Computer-Human Interaction* 15 (4): 1–21.

Youngman, Hennessy. 2011. "Hennessy Youngman on Relational Aesthetics." March 15. http://www.youtube.com/watch?v=7yea4qSJMx4&list=UU1kdURWGVjuksaqGK3oGoxA&index=11.

Index